Cambridge Elements 

Elements in Business Strategy
edited by
J.-C. Spender
Kozminski University

DIVERSIFICATION IN THE WORLD OF DATA AND AI

Gianvito Lanzolla
Bayes Business School

Constantinos Markides
London Business School

Shaftesbury Road, Cambridge CB2 8EA, United Kingdom

One Liberty Plaza, 20th Floor, New York, NY 10006, USA

477 Williamstown Road, Port Melbourne, VIC 3207, Australia

314–321, 3rd Floor, Plot 3, Splendor Forum, Jasola District Centre,
New Delhi – 110025, India

103 Penang Road, #05–06/07, Visioncrest Commercial, Singapore 238467

Cambridge University Press is part of Cambridge University Press & Assessment,
a department of the University of Cambridge.

We share the University's mission to contribute to society through the pursuit of
education, learning and research at the highest international levels of excellence.

www.cambridge.org
Information on this title: www.cambridge.org/9781009515832

DOI: 10.1017/9781009515801

When citing this work, please include a reference to the DOI 10.1017/9781009515801

First published 2025

A catalogue record for this publication is available from the British Library

ISBN 978-1-009-51583-2 Hardback
ISBN 978-1-009-51584-9 Paperback
ISSN 2515-0693 (online)
ISSN 2515-0685 (print)

Diversification in the World of Data and AI

Elements in Business Strategy

DOI: 10.1017/9781009515801
First published online: May 2025

Gianvito Lanzolla
Bayes Business School

Constantinos Markides
London Business School

Author for correspondence: Gianvito Lanzolla, g.lanzolla@city.ac.uk

Abstract: The datafication of digital reality and the diffusion of increasingly powerful AI systems have transformed the context within which diversification takes place, resulting in new realities for firms and necessitating new organizational capabilities. Building on their own field research and the existing literature on digitalization and diversification, the authors show how external technological and market changes influence the extent and type of diversification that firms can undertake. They argue that to succeed with digital diversification, new capabilities are needed and that these capabilities are not distributed evenly across firms. Only firms that possess these capabilities will undertake more diversification, with all other firms remaining focused. The authors finally argue that the necessary structures and the appropriate management of business units will differ from those used in the past because the digital context has brought to the fore new problems and risks for diversified firms. These are explored in this Element.

This Element also has a video abstract:
www.cambridge.org/EBUS_Lanzolla_abstract

Keywords: diversification, data and AI, conglomerates, ecosystems, corporate organisation

ISBNs: 9781009515832 (HB), 9781009515849 (PB), 9781009515801 (OC)
ISSNs: 2515-0693 (online), 2515-0685 (print)

Contents

1 Impact of the Digital Context on Theories of Diversification

Since the dawn of the digital age, in an apparent disregard of accepted wisdom, an increasing number of well-known companies have been diversifying into industries and markets that are totally unrelated to their core markets. Examples include Amazon's entry into the fitness market, Google's forays into banking, Tesla's moves into insurance, and Vodafone's attempts to enter the financial services market in the developing world. This behavior is reflected in the diversification indices of these firms. For example, Figure 1 shows the evolution of the Herfindahl-Hirschman Index (HHI) for Alphabet and Amazon in the period 2000–2020. Both companies show a decreasing HHI which suggests an increase in the scope of their diversification.

The recent flurry of unrelated diversification by companies such as Amazon and Alphabet seems surprising. Diversification into unrelated markets such as these would have spelled trouble for companies just twenty years ago. After a diversification boom in the 1960s and 1970s, the strategy of moving into unrelated markets fell into disrepute on Wall Street in the 1980s and conglomerates began commanding large diversification discounts (Campa and Kedia, 2002; Villalonga, 2004). This led to a refocusing wave, whereby diversified companies began selling off unrelated businesses in order to focus on their core (Markides, 1992, 1995). This was a time when unrelated diversification became synonymous with underperformance. It would take a brave company to go against accepted wisdom and in reality, not many of them do. As Figure 2 shows, the average HHI index for all S&P 500 companies has actually increased in the same time period, suggesting that many other firms are following accepted wisdom and are decreasing their diversification. What is it about firms such as Amazon and Alphabet that explains their drive toward *more* unrelated diversification?

This manuscript aims to address this puzzle and, in the process, explore the concept of diversification in the context of the digital era. Specifically, we aim to answer the questions: Does the digital revolution introduce any novel elements that alter the core principles of diversification and so explain the diversification behaviors of firms such as Amazon and Alphabet? If so, how?

1.1 The Received Wisdom on the Economics of Corporate Diversification

Over the past fifty years, since the seminal work of Penrose (1959) and Rumelt (1974, 1982), a rich literature on corporate diversification has developed. According to this literature, the fundamental principles that explain why firms engage in diversification are the following:

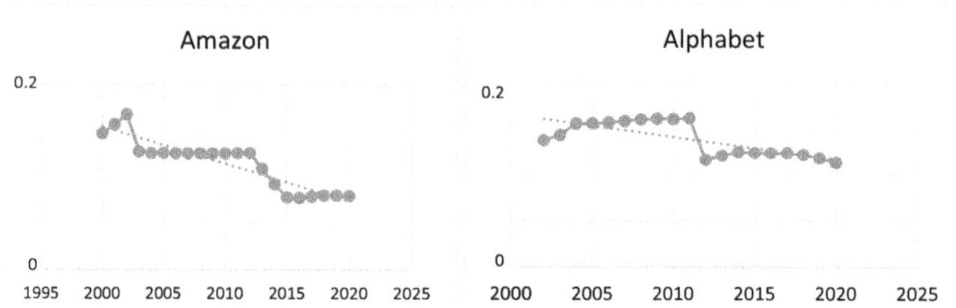

Figure 1 HHI for Amazon and Alphabet

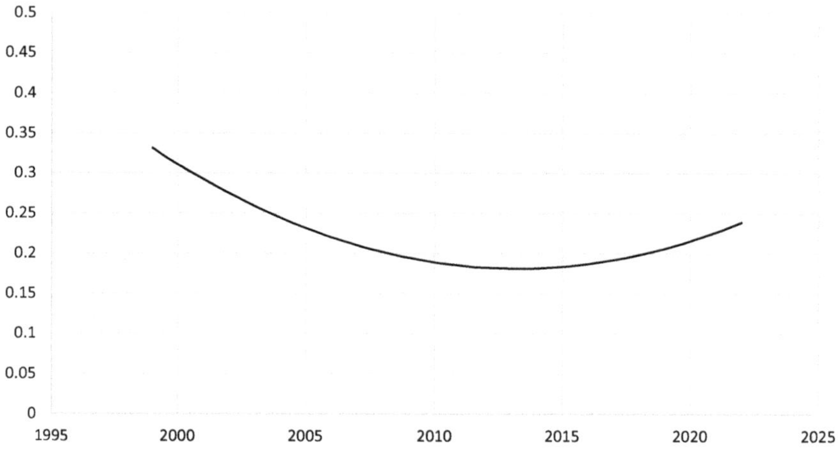

Figure 2 HHI polynomial trendline (S&P 500 sample)

- A company may possess surplus assets which are underutilized and not efficiently tradable in the open market.
- Unable to trade these assets, the company retains them and employs them internally in alternative markets.
- As the company employs these assets further from its core market, the utility derived from these assets diminishes. The assets were originally developed for a specific market, so the further the company moves away from this market, the weaker the alignment between the asset and the market, resulting in decreased productivity.
- At the same time, moving away from its core market increases coordination and transaction costs. This is due to the heightened complexity and management constraints associated with operating in distant markets.

Based on the extant economic logic, academics have argued that every firm has a limit to how much it can diversify (Markides, 1995). The argument goes as follows: the exploitation of underutilized assets and competences in new markets creates value for the firm. If the assets are utilized in a market that is close to the core market, they can be as productive as they were in their original use in the core market and so create a lot of value in the new market. If, on the other hand, they are applied in markets that are far away from the core, then their productivity declines because they are being used for something different from their original purpose. This suggests that the further a firm diversifies from its core business, the less value it can extract from its assets, a relationship shown as a declining marginal benefits curve in Figure 3. At the same time, these benefits to diversification are not achieved without cost. In fact, the further the firm diversifies from its core, the bigger the costs associated with managing all the different businesses under one corporate umbrella. The rising marginal cost curve in Figure 3 shows this relationship between the level of diversification and the costs of diversification. The point at which the marginal benefits and marginal costs curves meet is what is known as the "optimal" level of diversification for a given firm. A firm can create value through diversification if it diversifies up to this level but will destroy value if it tried to diversify beyond this level.

In what follows, we will argue that the digital revolution of the last twenty years has *not* changed this economic logic for diversification, but it has changed the context within which diversification now happens. Specifically, today's pervasive connectivity and ever-growing (cloud) computing power allow companies to leverage a new asset – data – as well as exploit AI, and ecosystems for their diversification strategies. This has resulted in different diversification dynamics, reflected in the company behaviors we observe.

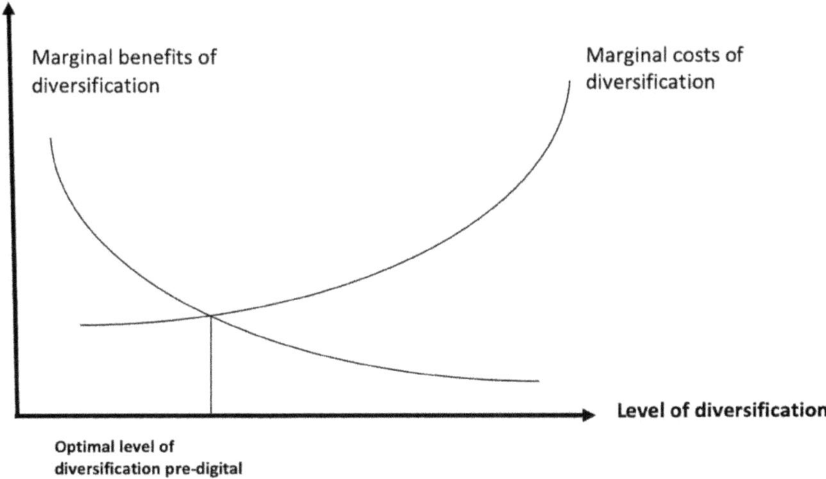

Figure 3 The marginal benefits and costs of diversification

1.2 The Digital Transformation of Physical Reality and the New Context for Diversification

The economic logic of diversification was developed in the institutional and technological context of the second half of the twentieth century. The increasing diffusion of digital technologies since 2000 has changed the context in which companies operate, something which is often referred to as digital transformation. What has been the effect of this change in context?

Digital technology is an umbrella term encompassing several general-purpose technologies – such as computer vision, sensors, the Internet of Things (IoT), artificial intelligence (AI), and cloud computing. Enabled by the diffusion of these technologies, the physical reality is being radically transformed, as shown in Figure 4. At the heart of this digital transformation of the physical reality is the process of sensing, or digitizing, which involves capturing physical actions, states, or representations and converting them into a digital data format. This process often involves using various sensors and devices to collect data from physical objects, measuring parameters such as temperature, pressure, motion, and environmental conditions.

Once sensed and digitized, these physical assets can communicate and connect with other digitized assets through the Internet of Things (IoT) or other communication technologies, such as edge computing and 5G. For instance, IoT technology enables the seamless exchange of information between interconnected devices, creating a network of "smart" assets that can interact with each other in real time.

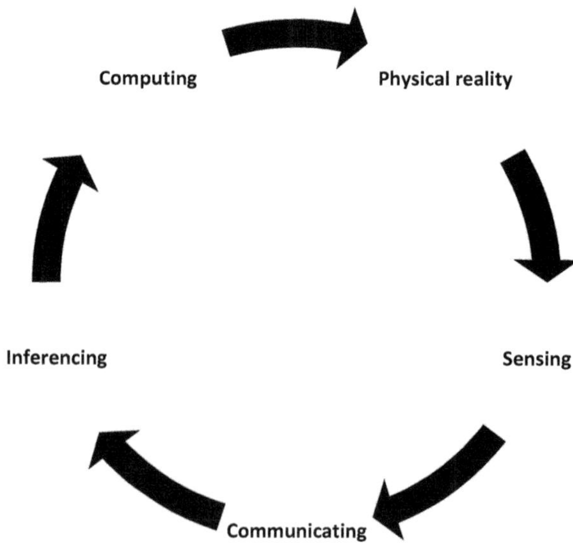

Figure 4 The digitalization of physical assets

The interconnected network of digitized assets generates vast amounts of data, often referred to as big data. This data is continuously collected, transmitted, and stored, providing a rich source of information for further analysis. The sheer volume and variety of data generated by these connected assets is overwhelming. For instance, in 2023, the world generated approximately 123 zettabytes of data. By 2028, the amount of data generated globally is expected to reach 394 zettabytes (Statista.com), marking a 220 percent increase from 2023. This upward trend does not seem to have an end, either.

To analyze this data, we can employ advanced inferencing systems such as artificial intelligence (AI) and machine learning (ML) algorithms. AI refers to the branch of computer science and engineering that focuses on the development of algorithms and systems capable of performing tasks that typically require human intelligence. These tasks encompass a broad spectrum, ranging from basic pattern recognition and problem-solving to more complex activities such as natural language understanding, decision-making, and autonomous reasoning. AI systems leverage techniques such as machine learning, neural networks, and natural language processing to simulate, virtualize, or augment the physical reality (Bailey et al., 2012; Porter and Heppelmann, 2017).

For example, the company John Deere utilizes a range of sensors placed on farming equipment and on farms to collect data on soil conditions, crop health, moisture levels, and weather conditions. The digital data is transmitted to John Deere's cloud-based platform, MyJohnDeere, where advanced analytics and machine learning algorithms process the data to generate actionable insights such as optimal planting times, fertilizer application rates, and irrigation schedules based on real-time and historical data.

AI and ML algorithms become more powerful as they process more data. At the same time, AI and ML are also significantly enhanced by advancements in computing technologies, particularly Cloud computing. Cloud computing provides the necessary infrastructure to store, process, and analyze large datasets efficiently. It offers scalable computing power and storage resources, enabling more complex and powerful AI applications. To put the scale of digital transformation into perspective, Statista estimates that spending on digital transformation reached $2.15 trillion in 2023. This figure is projected to rise to $3.9 trillion by 2027. Additionally, worldwide spending on AI-centric systems across all industries was estimated at $154 billion in 2023.

Thus far we have briefly described the technological foundation at the core of the digital transformation of the physical reality. The environmental, social, and business impacts of these changes have been analyzed by a large and growing literature which has outlined the intricacies of such transformations. For instance, Creutzig et al. (2022) note that "great claims have been made about the benefits of dematerialization in a digital economy." Yet, they also note that the net impact of digitalization on the environment, labor markets, resource use, governance, and power relationships depend on several interaction effects and human agency, making the outcome often unpredictable. Along the same lines, Lanzolla, Pesce, and Tucci (2021) show that the outcome of digitalization in enabling more efficient knowledge integration is far from being always positive.

As regards diversification, this digital transformation has resulted in four changes of interest:

* The digitalization of the physical reality creates data as a valuable new asset that diversifying firms can strategically leverage. What is unique about data in the digital age is that it is potentially so rich that it contains information that might be applicable in completely different industry contexts. In this sense, data is less (co)specialized with the legacy positioning of the company. This implies that data – in conjunction with AI which allows for the development of insights from this data – has higher potential than traditional fixed assets or traditional capabilities to create value in new markets. Data is a type of asset that can be transferred to far away markets without losing its beneficial effects as fast as other physical assets.
* Digital ecosystems mitigate the risks of executing strategies in areas beyond a company's traditional market positioning.
* Digital technology, such as algorithmic controls, facilitates reductions in coordination and control costs.
* The trading of data in markets is subject to inherent limitations.

We explore these four points in more detail next and then discuss their collective effect on diversification.

1.3 Data as a New Asset at the Heart of Diversification

The concept of data and information as strategic assets is not a new one. Stemming from the seminal works of Akerlof, Spence, and Stiglitz (who shared the Nobel Prize in 1970), academic research has highlighted the key features of information as a strategic asset. First, unlike physical resources, information is non-depletable, meaning it does not diminish with use. In other words, once information is created, it can be used repeatedly without being exhausted, and its value can increase as more people leverage it for various purposes. However, the value of information can diminish in terms of marginal utility: as more information is acquired, the incremental value or utility of additional information might decrease. Furthermore, the value of information can decline over time if it becomes outdated or irrelevant: information is most valuable when it is current and applicable to the context at hand. Finally, in markets, the value of information can decrease if it becomes too widely available: when proprietary or exclusive information becomes common knowledge, its competitive advantage diminishes.

What is new in the digital age is that the sheer **volume** of data generated and collected from various sources; the **velocity** at which data is generated; and the **variety** of this data can generate information of an unprecedented scope and scale (McAfee and Brynjolfsson, 2012). Furthermore, what is unique about data in the digital age is that it is potentially so rich that it contains information that might be applicable in completely different industry contexts.

Data for Increasing Efficiency in the Utilization of Physical Assets. Through their digital representation, a firm's physical assets can be monitored, measured, and analyzed in unprecedented detail. More specifically, through their digital artefacts, the physical assets acquire characteristics which are typical of software products (e.g., Yoo, 2010). For instance, they become more traceable and editable which facilitates the (continuous) improvement of any elements while maintaining logical structures intact. Like software, they also become more replicable, thus enabling the effortless reproduction and dissemination of digital artifacts at minimal marginal costs – for example, consider songs which can be replicated infinitely with negligible expenditure. Similarly, modularity plays a crucial role in the decomposition and reconstitution of digital elements, fostering collaboration and adaptability across varied contexts. Finally, the granularity inherent in digital artifacts facilitates the detailed analyses and manipulations of the physical asset and of the digital artefact alike. Overall, the digital artifacts related to the physical assets create new representations that impact the ways in which physical assets are used thus changing their utilization and efficiency. It follows that more efficient asset utilization might generate the excess capacity for more diversification.

Data as a Generative Asset for Deriving Insights about Value Creation (in Related or Unrelated Markets). Through the aggregation and scrutiny of different data sources alongside the utilization of artificial intelligence, firms can procure unique insights into assets and client behavior. The academic literature has identified several mechanisms for discovery, including data fusion and integration, which combines data from multiple sources to provide a comprehensive view and uncover new insights. Pattern recognition uses statistical techniques, machine learning, and data mining to reveal hidden patterns and correlations in large datasets. Hypothesis generation and iterative learning involve the analysis of data to generate hypotheses based on observed patterns, guiding further investigation through continuous testing, experimentation, and feedback to refine models and uncover deeper insights.

Such insights can be leveraged in several ways. For instance, the anticipation of needs and the customization of offerings can manifest in the capacity to cross-promote or upsell correlated products or services to extant clientele (Bharadwaj et al., 2013; Bughin et al., 2018; Zhu et al., 2016). At a more general level, when a firm possesses an understanding of its clientele's preferences, it can discern supplementary and more profound offerings that complement extant consumer utilization or acquisition, or it may endeavor to capture the life-cycle value of such clientele. Overall, the retention of contented clientele is comparatively less financially burdensome than the pursuit of new ones, particularly during the transition of clientele from mature products to next-generation alternatives (Bolton, 1998; Gupta and Zeithaml, 2006; Kumar and Reinartz, 2016; Rust, Lemon, and Zeithaml, 2004; Venkatesan and Kumar, 2004), thus providing a second advantage to companies that can leverage this mechanism.

The generation of new insights about drivers of value creation is not limited to a company's legacy positioning. For example, once Apple harvests behavioral data from its Apple watch wearers, it can analyze this data and develop insights about their nutrition, shopping, entertainment, or health. In other words, data collected via the Apple Watch is not restricted to the typical function of a watch. Similarly, once Netflix collects enough data on the types of movies its subscribers prefer, it can develop insights on viewers' preferences and "diversify" away from just streaming movies to also producing them. That such a strategy can succeed is evidenced from the fact that eight out of the ten most successful movies produced in China in 2019 were based on insights developed from patterns of preferences extracted from Alibaba's platform.

Data in conjunction with pervasive client accessibility has given rise to what some authors call demand-side diversification (Harrigan, 2023) whereby companies seek customer-based synergies rather than production-related synergies. In this light, diversification is aimed at offering a broader value proposition through additions to existing product lines (Adner and Zemsky, 2006; Schmidt, Madadok, and Keil, 2016). Amazon's vision of "[being] Earth's most customer-centric company, where customers can find and discover anything they might want to buy online, and endeavors to offer its customers the lowest possible prices" is a fitting example of such demand-side dynamics whereby customer data and customer base reinforce each other to create an even broader value proposition. The already cited cases of Apple (entering healthcare and entertainment) and Tesla (entering insurance) are other textbook examples of such dynamics. Manral and Harrigan (2018a and 2018b) find that this approach often increases the firms' unrelated-diversification scores while maintaining high customer-similarity ratios.

Data as the Shaper of a New Ontology. Finally, some scholars have even hypothesized that the digitalization of physical reality fundamentally alters reality's ontology, too. Baskerville et al. (2020) coined the term "ontological reversal," indicating that digital versions often precede their physical counterparts, seen in practices like 3-D printing. This shift redefines product production, with digital versions taking priority over physical ones. Traditionally, physical objects served as the basis for digital representations, but ontological reversal suggests the opposite, challenging notions of materiality. For example, digital records stored in the cloud increasingly replace physical tickets, becoming the primary proof of transaction. Ontological reversal extends beyond digitization, fundamentally restructuring reality where digital entities hold greater significance. This has profound implications across commerce, communication, and identity. In commerce, digital products may outweigh physical ones due to scalability and accessibility. Similarly, digital identities and communities may overshadow traditional social connections, reshaping interpersonal dynamics. Furthermore, it blurs temporal and spatial boundaries, making the distinction between "real" and "digital" more fluid. Traditional diversification strategies focus on physical and financial assets. With ontological reversal, data becomes perhaps the only asset, systematically altering how companies assess value and potential diversification opportunities.

1.4 Digital Technology for Reducing Strategy Execution Risks, Costs of Coordination and Costs of Control

A second significant shift lies in the structure and governance of strategy execution. Unlike diversifiers of the past, today's digital diversifiers no longer need to handle everything on their own. In the past, companies had to build and manage a wide range of capabilities internally, leading to inefficiencies and slower response times. They invested heavily in infrastructure, research and development, and workforce training to diversify. This approach often limited the speed and scope of diversification efforts. The digital context has transformed this paradigm. By enabling companies to engage with a broader and more diverse array of partners, digital ecosystems allow companies to leverage external partnerships and collaborations, accessing specialized knowledge and innovative solutions without developing these capabilities internally (Adner, 2017; Baldwin, 2004; Jacobides, Cessano, and Gawer, 2018; Lanzolla and Markides, 2022). For instance, extant research has shown how different collaborative arrangements between innovators and complementors influence their ability to invest in new technology and commercialize it (e.g., Kapoor and Lee, 2013; Leten et al., 2013); how knowledge sharing affects inter-firm relationships and ecosystem development (e.g., Alexy, George, and Salter, 2013; Brusoni and Prencipe, 2013; Frankort, 2013); and the overall health and longevity of the ecosystem (e.g., Leten et al., 2013), and the strategy and management of partnerships in digital ecosystems (Lanzolla and Markides, 2022).

An increase in the number and variety of partners to execute strategy might be beneficial but might also be subject to higher coordination and control costs. In the received theory of diversification, coordination and control costs are considered as a barrier to diversification as complexity increases. However, the digital contexts provide also a second fundamental shift in governance logics (Bailey et al., 2019; Barrett et al., 2012; Baum and Haveman, 2020; Brynjolfsson and McAfee, 2014; Cohen and Tripsas, 2018; Faraj et al., 2011; Lee and Berente, 2012) which significantly affect coordination costs. This shift is enabled by digital technologies which are often described under the label of algorithmic controls (Kellogg et al., 2020). Algorithmic controls involve the deployment of sophisticated algorithms and machine learning techniques to automate and optimize decision-making and (inter)organizational governance. Algorithmic controls represent a departure from traditional modes of organizational control and decision-making, introducing novel approaches that leverage computational power and data-driven insights to inform and guide managerial actions.

By harnessing the capabilities of AI and advanced analytics, organizations can achieve greater efficiency, accuracy, and agility in their operations, enabling them to adapt more effectively to dynamic and complex environments. The adoption of algorithmic controls facilitates real-time monitoring, analysis, and optimization of organizational processes, allowing for proactive decision-making and strategic adaptation in response to changing market conditions and competitive pressures. Algorithmic controls have far-reaching implications for organizational dynamics, power structures, and employee behaviors. As decision-making authority becomes increasingly delegated to algorithms and automated systems, questions arise concerning accountability, transparency, and ethical governance (Kellogg et al., 2020). Additionally, the reliance on algorithmic recommendations and predictions may influence managerial perceptions, attitudes, and behaviors, potentially shaping organizational cultures and norms (Faraj et al., 2011).

Pervasive Connectivity and Network Effects. Network effects occur when a product or service becomes more valuable to a user as more people use it. The value increase relative to the number of users is often depicted as a "quadratic" function. Consequently, establishing network effects (NE) becomes a powerful mechanism for customer lock-in. While NE is not an economic force unique to the digital age, the ubiquity of connectivity in the digital context allows NE to be established across broader and more diverse user bases, encompassing varied demographics, regions, and preferences.

Received wisdom would suggest that establishing NE is easier when products are based on open standards and market mechanisms. For example, the Android operating system, which is open source, allows various manufacturers to create devices that can seamlessly interact with each other, thus leveraging open standards to establish widespread network effects. The digital context, for the relevance of data as the driver of value creation and for providing stronger internal control/coordination mechanisms, might provide strong economic advantages to companies that internalize the delivery of several complementary assets around a central value proposition.

For instance, Boudreau, Jeppesen, and Miric (2021) explored how network effects impacted firms using freemium strategies in the Apple App Store, finding that network effects alone do not boost revenues, but combined with freemium models, they enhance market leaders' dominance. The study showed that while freemium strategies can expand user bases and leverage network effects, they may also reduce revenues for followers and reinforce market leaders' positions, suggesting platform owners must carefully consider the broader market implications.

One textbook example that illustrates this mechanism is Apple's approach with its ecosystem. Despite the dominance of open standards, Apple has successfully internalized the delivery of several complementary assets around a central value proposition – its ecosystem of devices and services. Apple's iOS, macOS, watchOS, and other software are tightly integrated with its hardware products like the iPhone, MacBook, Apple Watch, and AirPods. Apple's internal mechanisms counterbalance the power of open standards and market forces.

Xiaomi's diverse product portfolio, encompassing smartphones, electronics, IoT devices, and software, highlights its strategic approach to diversification. By leveraging extensive user data, fostering engaged community participation, and building an integrated ecosystem of products and services, Xiaomi enhances customer satisfaction while effectively reducing risks associated with entering new markets and product categories.

1.5 Trading Data versus Exploiting Data through Diversification

According to the theory of diversification, excess capacity might be sold in open markets, and diversification occurs only when such commercial transactions are not possible or economically advantageous. Thus far, we have established that data is at the core of diversification in the digital age. The related question, therefore, is: "what are the considerations related to trading data versus exploiting data internally?"

Companies such as Apple, Amazon, Facebook, and Google often monetize the data they collect by providing access to third parties or directly selling it (Manyika et al., 2011). However, not all data can be traded. In the context of data commerce, it is essential to distinguish between data and information goods, with our focus primarily on the former. Despite the potential economic value inherent in data, several factors impede their tradability and integration into third-party business models. Notably, considerations such as data quality, compliance with regulations, and the ability to appropriate value from data assets pose significant challenges (Koutroumpis et al., 2020).

Integrating data into a company's value proposition represents a complex endeavor, burdened with both technological and managerial hurdles (Lanzolla and Markides, 2022). The absence of a ubiquitous "eBay for data" marketplace can be attributed to formidable concerns regarding strategic behaviors, data quality assurance, and the lack of sufficient control over the utilization of data by prospective buyers (Thomas, Leiponen, and Koutroumpis, 2020). Furthermore, a significant portion of the data amassed in contemporary digital environments falls under the category of "exhaust data," originating as by-products of various online activities such as e-commerce transactions and social interactions, rather than being intentionally generated for analytical purposes (Manyika et al., 2011; Mayer-Schonberger and Cukier, 2013).

Finally, the information paradox, articulated by economist Kenneth Arrow (1974, 1985), significantly limits the trading of data in open markets. This paradox highlights the dilemma where the buyer needs to know the value of the data before purchasing it, but once the buyer knows the information, there is no need to buy it. This creates a value assessment dilemma, as sellers are hesitant to reveal too much about their data for fear of it being used without compensation, while buyers are reluctant to purchase data without understanding its worth. Additionally, risks of data leakage and intellectual property theft further discourage detailed disclosures from sellers. This leads to trust and verification challenges, where buyers need assurance of data quality and relevance without full access, complicating the establishment of fair pricing and efficient market transactions.

1.6 Toward a New Theory of Diversification in the Digital Age?

Table 1 summarizes the differences between the theory of traditional diversification and data-driven diversification in the digital age, as discussed thus far.

Our discussion thus far – allows us to generate insights on how diversification is affected by the digital context. First, the marginal benefits curve has shifted upward primarily because firms are now increasingly using

Table 1 Diversification in the digital age

	Traditional theory	**Data-driven diversification**
Drivers of diversification	• Excess capacity in physical assets	• Data volume, variety and velocity • Artificial intelligence
Characteristics of the assets driving diversification	• Physical assets are finite • Benefits decrease with distance from the initial context of asset deployment	• Data is generative and (more) independent from legacy positioning • Data is scalable and easy to customize • Data and connectivity trigger pervasive network effects
Cost of diversification	• Costs increase exponentially with complexity	• Digital ecosystems and algorithmic controls and digital ecosystems decrease coordination costs
Limitations for asset trading	• To limit IP discovery • Transaction costs • Integration in buyer's business model	• Information paradox • Data privacy • Integration in buyer's technological infrastructure

data to diversify. What is unique about data as an asset is that it contains information that might be applicable in completely different industry contexts. In this sense, data is less (co)specialized with the legacy positioning of the company. This implies that data – in conjunction with AI which allows for the development of insights from this data – has higher potential than traditional fixed assets or traditional capabilities to create value in new markets. Data is a type of asset that can be transferred to far away markets without losing its beneficial effects as fast as other physical assets do. The end result of using this type of asset to diversify is that the marginal benefits curve of diversification has shifted upward. We show this in Figure 5.

At the same time, the costs associated with diversification have now been lowered through the use of AI and ecosystems. In contrast to diversifiers of old, today's diversifiers can diversify increasingly through partnerships. The reason

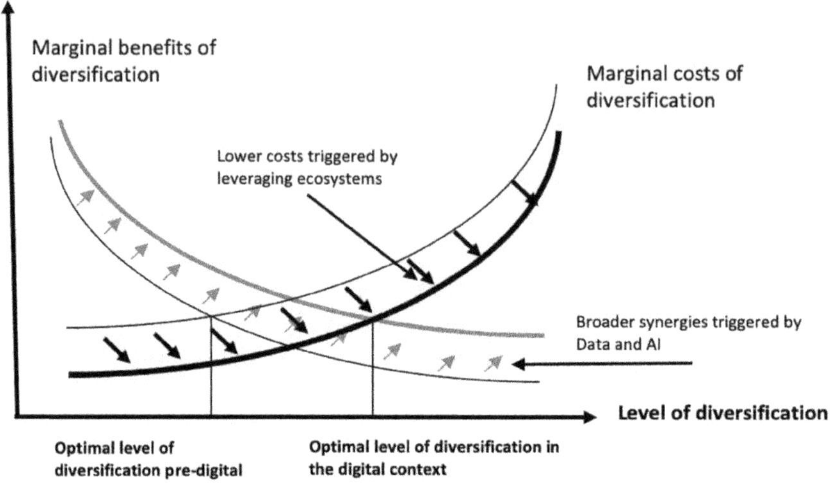

Figure 5 The marginal benefits and costs of diversification for digital diversifiers

for this is that in the digital context, connectivity and automation increase the availability and type of potential partners while decreasing coordination costs. For example, Apple can move into healthcare without having to make the products itself. It can subcontract manufacturing to a medical device manufacturer. Similarly, Google can enter the banking industry without having to "manufacture" bank accounts by itself – it can do it in alliance with traditional lenders. Likewise, Vodafone can move into banking in Africa, but it does not have to manufacture and sell banking products itself. It can subcontract these activities to partners in its ecosystem. It's not that this option was not available to diversifiers in the past, but the digital context has made it a more attractive option now. Not having to do everything under the same organizational hierarchy, in conjunction with the fact that coordination and control can be increasingly automated through AI, means that firms can now diversify without incurring the same: (a) coordination costs and (b) execution costs that previous diversifiers had to incur. This has resulted in the "cost" curve of diversification shifting downward – something shown in Figure 5.

The combined effect of the marginal benefits curve shifting upward and the marginal cost curve shifting downward is a new optimal level of diversification for firms. This optimal level is higher than what it used to be, suggesting that firms can now diversify much more than what they could twenty years ago. This explains why companies are now busily considering diversifying into seemingly unrelated businesses again.

2 Capabilities for Successful Diversification in the Digital Era

In the previous section, we argued that the digital revolution of the last twenty years has *not* changed the economic logic for diversification, but has changed the context within which diversification now takes place *in two fundamental ways*. First, rather than use traditional assets such as technology or brands to diversify, today's digital diversifiers can leverage a new asset to do so, specifically data. What is unique about data as an asset is that it contains information that might be applicable in completely different industry contexts. In this sense, data is less (co)specialized with the legacy positioning of the company. This implies that companies can diversify to markets that are far away from their core because data can be transferred to these far away markets without losing its beneficial effects as fast as other physical assets. Second, today's aspiring diversifiers can manage their portfolio of businesses through ecosystem partners. This is because in the digital context, connectivity and automation increase the availability and type of potential partners while decreasing coordination costs. This is important because not having to do everything under the same organizational hierarchy, in conjunction with the fact that coordination and control can be increasingly automated through AI, means that firms can now diversify without incurring the same coordination and execution costs that previous diversifiers had to incur (Aversa and Hueller, 2023). As argued in the previous section, the combination of these two changes brought about by the digital revolution has resulted in firms being able to diversify much more than before.

Being able to diversify more does not mean that everybody can do it successfully. It is only the companies that can exploit these two changes – more data and more partners – that will succeed with their diversification moves. And to exploit them successfully, certain capabilities are needed. First, there is the capability to collect the necessary data and, more importantly to generate value-creating insights out of it. Second, there is the capability to manage ecosystem partners in a digital context. We explore these factors next.

2.1 The Capability to Develop Constant Flows of Data in Context

In the course of doing business, companies collect a wealth of data on their assets, products, and customers. Very often, this data can provide information that may be useful in a *different* market from the one the company is operating in. For example, knowing how customers drive their cars gives Tesla the opportunity to develop insights on how to produce customized insurance products that incorporate these customers' driving behaviors. Similarly, having data on what movies their customers are watching can help Netflix develop insights as to what movies to make. Possession of this data may give diversifying companies an advantage over companies that do not have access to this data.

This advantage may be big enough to outweigh the advantages that incumbents have in the market the new entrant is moving into.

Therefore, the first ingredient for success is not just the possession of data but rather the possession of *data in context*. By this we mean data that captures people or asset behaviors in contexts relevant to the market where a firm may consider entering. For example, knowing what the customer buys in a supermarket or when they buy does not give that supermarket any insights about their movie preferences. This might explain why the British supermarket TESCO failed in its attempts to offer its customers video-on-demand services through its 2011 acquisition of Blinkbox. On the other hand, knowing how their customers drive their cars gives Tesla insights on how to develop customized insurance products that incorporate their driving behaviors.

Before a company can even consider a new market entry, it must create *flows* of data in context. This is not easy. The company first needs to have the appropriate infrastructure to capture this kind of data. More fundamentally, it needs to have the trust of clients as well as other industry stakeholders who will provide it with access and permission to use this data. This can be a formidable challenge.

Consider, first, the challenge of developing the appropriate infrastructure to capture data in context. Apple is quietly yet relentlessly building the infrastructure to capture people's health and fitness data, something often called "life-logging." For example, in September 2018, Apple launched an app that could detect when people fall down. In March 2019, it enabled the pairing of its devices with Snoww, Nike, QuardioArm (a smart blood pressure monitor) and DexCom Glucose (a glucose monitoring system). In June 2019, it improved the Apple GymKit app to include pairing with many more cardio equipment manufactured worldwide. It also launched a Cycle tracker for women and a Noise app to help users understand noise levels in high-risk environments. In June 2020, sleep trackers and automatic hand wash detectors were added to the Apple Watch, while, in September 2020, Apple Watch S6 incorporated blood oxygen sensors. These are all examples that highlight Apple's ambition in collecting data that can be leveraged in the healthcare market. Google's acquisition of FitBit and Amazon's release of the Halo band (that allows for the collection of customer data through wearables) show that the healthcare industry is very much an industry of interest to these two companies as well (Guardian, 2022; McKenna, 2021; Mishra and Dastin, 2022).

In addition to having the right kind of infrastructure to collect data in context, companies also need the trust of consumers to allow them access to this data. If Apple can collect data on consumers' health through its smartwatch, it can utilize this data to move into the healthcare market. But it is not only customer trust that is needed. To offer a good enough product, the new entrant may also need data that other industry participants – including competitors – have. Gaining trust with stakeholders is not easy. The example of the UK Ministry of Justice is a case in point. Despite putting together the right infrastructure – digital bracelets on convicted felons – it proved very difficult for the UK Ministry of Justice (MoJ) to collect "data in context" from them. According to Arif Harbott, the CIO at the MoJ in 2017, the convicts simply did not "trust" the MoJ to deal with their data and did everything to interfere with the proper functioning of their bracelets.

Appropriate infrastructure and the trust of clients as well as other stakeholders to collect and use this data are both of paramount importance for building flows of data in context, and often create self-reinforcing, or self-destructing loops vis-à-vis building flows of data in context. The example of GE's Predix is a case in point. On paper, GE had both a remarkable budget for building the Predix infrastructure and clients who seemed willing to share data to get better service and optimize their operations. According to a senior GE executive intimately involved in the development of Predix, the idea behind it – at least on paper – was brilliant. In his words:

> *GE had trillions of dollars' worth of assets installed around the world. We had to think how to make these assets more productive before anybody else did. This led to Predix. The idea was to build a digital platform, bring partners in and build an ecosystem. By digitalizing and connecting our industrial assets (such as jet engines, industrial plants and locomotives), we can generate data on each asset that would then enable all kinds of predictions and service personalization. For example, instead of taking 3 weeks to service a jet engine, we can now predict when a single blade in the engine needs servicing or replacing.*

Jeff Immelt, the CEO of GE at the time, bet the company and its legacy on this vision. Yet, Jeff Immelt's plan to make GE a top ten software company by 2020 did not materialize. There are several reasons for this failure, but the biggest were the platform infrastructure's failure to deliver and the subsequent breakdown in stakeholders' trust. A senior executive commented that "*it quickly became apparent that the APIs (that allow an application to access the data) and the microservices developed for the platform were unable to collect data correctly.*" This created problems for the GE partners (such as application software developers) who had built applications to analyze this data and generate insights for their clients. They had difficulties accessing this data properly and even worse, could not trust its reliability. It wasn't long before they started complaining about technical problems and delays. A tipping point was reached when GE asked its partners for a two-month "break" to fix these problems. This undermined GE's credibility further because its partners could not allow their resources to sit idle for two months. Relations were further undermined when former GE Digital CEO Bill Ruh declared in August 2017 that from that moment on "our resources will go to our fastest-selling markets," a clear signal of a shift in strategy. In the end, the erosion of trust between GE and its partners spelled the demise of Predix's initial grand vision.

Big Tech platforms – the likes of Amazon, Google, Facebook, and Apple – have a clear advantage to build flows of data in context. Not only is the platform infrastructure fit-for purpose for pervasive data collection but some of these platforms have grown to become trusted brands, with both clients and broader stakeholders.

2.2 The Capability to Generate Insights from Data by Blending AI and Domain Expertise

Having flows of data in context is a good start. But this alone is not enough. What a new entrant needs to do is to convert this data into viable and scalable ideas that differentiate it relative to the established players in the market it is entering. The incumbents may not have the data the entrant has, but they have numerous other advantages simply on the basis that they have been operating in that market long before the potential entrant. To succeed with new market entry, a firm needs to leverage its data advantage in a creative way so as to give itself a fighting chance against the incumbents. This implies that entry might be a bad move even when the potential entrant has a data advantage over incumbents.

For example, consider the case of Sky UK. The company has installed millions of satellite dishes across the UK over the past twenty-five years. The signal received by these satellite dishes is affected by weather patterns, offering Sky the opportunity to collect highly granular real-time weather data across the UK. The company's management knew that the weather data they had been collecting was valuable, and they considered the possibility to use this data to enter several new markets such as insurance, clothing, energy, and even umbrella selling. Yet, they decided against entering any of these markets primarily because they realized that having the necessary data was not enough to give them a competitive advantage or make them successful in these markets. On the other hand, Netflix decided to expand beyond content streaming to content production. They did so because they found a way to leverage their data in context to achieve a competitive advantage over other content producers. The flows of data in context collected from their large customer base allows Netflix to develop content that is informed by a deep "real time" understanding of their viewers' tastes.

Converting data into customized insights is not easy. Simply analyzing the data or using AI algorithms to identify patterns in the data is almost never enough. For example, Universal Music possesses detailed data about people's music preferences. They further enrich this data by combining it with additional insights on people's habits, behaviors, and preferences that they display through their activities on social media. The combination has produced a data pool that is so huge that the company has created a dedicated division whose responsibilities include exploring this data to extract business value for artists and partners. The potential of this flows of data is high and has already materialized in new market entries spanning from the launch of a new hotel chain (UMusic Hotel) to pizza delivery (Gangstarella Pizza). Yet, according to Olivier Robert-Murphy, Executive Vice President at Universal Music Group for Brands: "... *extracting/ capturing insights that create value is not straightforward and requires the development of brand-new capabilities.*"

Another example is the UK Meteorological Office (hereafter, Met Office). The Met Office had a lot of granular data about the weather, as well as the most powerful computing capabilities and state of the art AI experts. They could use these capabilities to develop services for a number of industries. For example, they could advise airliners such as British Airways the best route to take on any given flight to avoid weather turbulence or head winds. They could also offer consulting services to transportation companies such as Maersk as well as farmers and other agricultural workers. According to the Met Office's CIO, Charles Ewen, they did experiment with a few of these services – such as advising airliners on route selection that optimized fuel consumption. Yet, after a few initial attempts, the Met Office decided to abandon its forays in these areas.

According to Ewen: "*What the Met Office realized was that mastering weather forecasts is only one ingredient for success in offering services such as crop selection or fuel optimization, to farmers or airlines.*" The other ingredient is having *domain expertise* in the various markets they were entering – which the Met Office did not have. As a result, Ewen said that "*[the Met Office] decided to focus even more on the core business of making meteorological predictions alongside developing our competencies in collaboration and partnerships with domain experts.*"

The mistake companies often make is to assume that building an AI infrastructure and hiring lots of AI experts will allow them to deliver on their data advantage. AI is invaluable for automating and scaling but using some machine learning algorithm to identify patterns in the data will rarely deliver the creative insights that a company needs to outsmart the incumbents in the markets it is entering. AI experts may master automation but often lack the knowledge and experience to contextualize the insights. The lack of contextualization may prove costly. It is the fusion of AI expertise with domain expertise that underpins the capability that allow for the delivery of customized insights at scale. Many companies do not have the domain expertise in the markets they wish to enter. For example, Apple has made no secret of its desire to move into the healthcare industry. Its CEO, Tim Cook, recently described the healthcare industry as an area where the company could make a "meaningful impact" for humanity. But Apple lacks the domain expertise – it knows very little about the healthcare business. If it is to succeed in this new market, it will need the help of partners that have the necessary expertise. For example, it has recently partnered with Stanford Medicine to conduct a study with over 400,000 participants from all 50 states in the span of 8 months.

Alphabet's Waymo faced a similar challenge. There is no doubt that Alphabet's Waymo has a pool of the best AI scientists in its autonomous vehicles' projects. But to exploit its technology in the car industry, it needs domain expertise. Its recently departed leader, John Krafcik, is a former auto industry executive, who brought his industry experience into the equation. In addition, Mr. Krafcik has put the company on a path of increasing partnerships with auto companies such as Daimler and FCA to help them merge their huge data pool and cloud/AI capabilities with industry expertise.

Netflix is another example of a company that uses industry experts to help it. Insights from viewing behaviors are not simply translated into new production scripts. Such insights are used as input factors to identify trending patterns but then the probing and the production of the scripts is delegated to script writers: AI cannot yet write scripts. Traditional television players such as the BBC found it increasingly more difficult to compete because the likes of Apple, Amazon, and Netflix were hiring script writers and content producers at sky-high salaries, at a level unseen in the industry.

Blending AI and domain expertise is crucial, yet not easy. After he left GE, Jeff Immelt candidly admitted that what he got wrong was thinking that the success of Predix was only based on technology and AI. The integration of GE Digital into GE Energy and the embedding of AI capabilities in the new companies – GE aviation and GE Healthcare – show once again the importance of fusing AI and domain expertise to generate useful insights from data. This hard-learned lesson was recently summarized in GE's new mantra: "to understand the insights hidden in data: process engineers don't have to be a data scientist." This was a point also emphasized by Giordano Albertazzi, President of Europe, Middle East, and Africa at Vertiv, a critical infrastructure provider. He said:

> *[...] integrating AI experts and engineers is not easy. Yet, onboarding AI experts and domain expertise in the same team, with similar objectives helps in generating insights needed for expanding and elevating our value proposition. Overall, we have learned that in the b2b space the expansion should be led by industry experts, augmented by AI experts, not the other way round. What is crucial for successful value expansion is uncompromised understanding of customer needs and not reinventing the wheel.*

2.3 The Capability to Manage Ecosystem "Partners" in the Digital Context

The blending of AI and domain expertise helps to develop bespoke insights, but to succeed in the new market, the company needs to deliver on its value proposition. For this to happen, many other capabilities are needed, and the company needs to decide on how to acquire or develop these additional capabilities. Fortunately, the digital context has made this task a little easier for potential new entrants: there are now many more potential partners with whom they can partner to execute their strategies. There is no question that digital connectivity has provided companies with many more partners to work with in order to enter and compete in new markets (Jacobides, Cennamo, and Gawer, 2018).

For example, in an effort to become a software industry champion and boost adoption of Predix, GE launched a Global Digital Alliance Program in 2016 which was " ... *dedicated to building the digital industrial ecosystem across global systems integrators, independent software vendors, telecommunications service providers and technology providers.*" According to a GE top executive: "*We were able to sign 464 partners in a single year. The ecosystem (strategy advisors, software integrators, software houses, hardware companies, etc) literally jumped at us. Predix had the potential to build a multibillion-dollar market for all and they all wanted a piece of the pie.*"

Axel Springer, the German media company, now operates a very successful portfolio of online digital classified businesses, including the job portal StepStone and property sites such as Immonet. A senior executive at Axel Springer acknowledged that they have been able to enter into these new markets without having to build all these different businesses. As he put it: "*We do not have to be the providers of these products. We simply have to find the best providers and connect them to customers through our platform.*"

It is therefore noncontroversial to propose that companies today have a wide choice of potential partners to work with in the new markets they enter. This, however, has given rise to a new challenge for firms: not all of these partners contribute equally to the relationship. This is important because different types of partners require different approaches from the digital diversifier. How can a firm determine what type of partner is needed and what kind of challenges it will face in managing each type?[1]

The answer to this question will be greatly influenced by two key factors:

- the partner's contribution in offering *data in context* to the new entrant; and

---

[1] The section that follows was originally published as: Gianvito Lanzolla and Constantinos Markides. "How to choose the right ecosystem partners for your business," HBR Online, March 28, 2022. Reprinted here by permission of *Harvard Business Review.*

- the partner's contribution in helping the new market entrant compete in an entirely new market.

Leveraging of data in context is critical for digital diversifiers. As argued already, data in context is not just any data – it is, instead, data that captures people or asset behaviors in contexts relevant to the market where a firm may consider entering. It is this data that gives the new entrant unique insights on what to offer the customers in the new market that even the established players in that market do not possess. A potential partner can add enormous value to the entrant by providing it with data in context that complements what the entrant already possesses. However, the data in context provided by a partner can vary in importance from being marginal to being of essence to the value proposition of the new entrant. For example, the data that Apple's app developers offer to Apple are of peripheral value to Apple. By contrast, the data that Predix's clients provide GE are absolutely essential to what GE Predix is trying to do – without this data, Predix has little valuable to offer.

The second area where a partner can add value is in helping the digital diversifier operate in the new market at scale, quickly and efficiently. For example, the partner can develop and manufacture the products that the entrant intends to offer, sparing the entrant the need to develop its own manufacturing operations and capabilities. The partner may also contribute in other ways by, for example, offering distribution and marketing services to the entrant or providing quick access to a large customer base. As was the case with data in context, the value that a partner brings to the operations of the new entrant can vary in importance from limited to significant. For example, farmers may provide John Deere with valuable data for it to develop new services but apart from that, they are not involved in how John Deere operates. By contrast, the car companies that partner with Waymo in the driverless car market will help Waymo not only with valuable data but also with the manufacture and distribution of these cars.

Putting these two factors together provides us with a classification scheme for what kind of partners each new entrant may need. This is shown in Table 2. The two dimensions of the table are the two areas that the partner can contribute to the entrant – data in context (on the vertical axis) and contributions in creating value in the new market (on the horizontal axis). The contributions in each of these areas can go from Low to High. This produces the 2X2 matrix shown in Table 2.

In the upper-left quadrant, we have partners that can be labeled as *satellites* – the data they offer to the new entrant is marginal and so is the support they can offer to the operations of the entrant. Apple's developers can be classified as such. In the upper-right quadrant, we have partners that can be called *complementors* – they offer limited or marginal data in context, but they provide

Table 2 How digital diversifiers can classify their partners

		Partners' contribution in helping the digital diversifier compete in the new market	
		Limited or in a few areas	**Significant and in many areas**
Partners' Contribution in offering data in context to the digital diversifier	*Data that is marginal or peripheral to the diversifier's value proposition in the new market*	Q1. *Satellites* (e.g., App developers for Apple or farmers to John Deere).	Q2. *Complementors* (e.g., script writers for Netflix; insurance companies for Tesla; banks for Google).
	Data that is of key essence to the diversifier's value proposition in the new market	Q3. *Suppliers* (e.g., some partners of GE Predix, pharmacies for Amazon; Met office for airline companies)	Q4. *Strategic partners* (e.g., Waymo and car companies that supply not only cars but the means to collect data. A few of the GE Predix partners).

significant support to the new entrant in running its operations in the new market. The script writers for Netflix or the insurance companies that will help Tesla develop and sell customized insurance policies to Tesla drivers are examples of complementors. Salesforce's ecosystem provides another example. If we make 100 the total value delivered through Salesforce's platform, complementors such as system integrators and specialized app developers contribute a significant part of this value, some say up to 80 percent (with the remaining 20 percent contributed by Salesforce itself).

In the bottom-left quadrant, we have partners that can be called *suppliers* – they provide valuable data in context but little else. The UK Meteorological Office (Met office) is a good example of such a supplier, offering its meteorological data to consultancies to develop services for their customers. Finally, in the bottom-right quadrant, we have partners that can be called *strategic partners* – they provide both data in context that is of critical importance to the new entrant but also services and support that the diversifier needs to operate in the new market. The car companies partnering with Waymo can be classified as such.

This classification shows that there are different types of "partners" with whom a digital diversifier can cooperate with and that treating them all as one and the same will be a mistake. Some of the recent work on digital ecosystems has failed to make the simple, yet important, point, that not all partners are the same. Although leveraging digital ecosystems is a common thread for all new market entrants, the argument here is that successful market entrants need to be clear about the role that their ecosystem partners have in their value proposition and differentiate their partner strategy accordingly. As Jose Salas, Global Head Strategic Alliances & Partnerships at Wolters Kluwer, commented: " . . . everybody uses the word partner, but they mean very different things. Be clear about what you need a partner for before devising your partnership management approach." Being able to identify the right partners is the key to a constructive working relationship and can be the difference between success and failure in new market entry.

2.3.1 Different Partners Create Different Partnership Management Challenges

The classification provided in Table 2 is useful in differentiating the various partners that a firm may need or have in its ecosystem. This, in turn, should lead to a better definition of the appropriate partnership strategy that the firm may need to develop – such as how many and what type of partners to ally with. At the same time, it should alert the company to the need to develop different relationship strategies for its different partners. The relationship strategy that it should adopt toward a satellite partner will almost certainly be different to the strategy that it should adopt toward a complementor or a strategic partner. The need to develop customized management approaches for its various partners is a new and unique challenge for firms. To make matters worse, the digital context has made the management of these partnerships even more complex and challenging than those in the pre-digital era – especially in areas such as managing one's reputation in high visibility environments; delivering on technological integration; and writing and enforcing contracts. We describe a few of these challenges below and summarize them in Table 3.

When dealing with *satellite partners*, the key challenge is often to create and maintain trust in conditions of high-power asymmetry. An example of how difficult this can be is the recent formation of the Coalition for App Fairness by Spotify, Epic Games, Blix, Tile, Match Group, and Basecamp to ask Apple for fairer fees on purchases happening through the Apple Store. In September 2020, following the high visibility of these claims, Apple introduced several policy changes, such as removing its 30 per cent fee on certain purchases which go through the Apple Store. In managing asymmetric relationships, managers should keep in mind the importance of reciprocity. This does not come naturally to managers of larger companies that are dealing with several satellite partners. Yet, breaching reciprocity might be very costly.

When dealing with *complementors*, the key challenge is often managing the firm's reputation or brand image. Doing so in the dynamic and highly transparent environment that the digital context has created is extra challenging and the risk that the actions of a partner in the ecosystem might damage the diversifier's brand is quite high. For example, according to senior executives at Nespresso, the company had repeatedly resisted entering into digital ecosystems for fear that its brand could be associated with "unwanted" third-party brands. Another well-known example here is Alibaba. Alibaba's TMall relies heavily on Merchants. For instance, it currently has more than 50,000 of them. From 2010 onward, Alibaba has been repeatedly accused of not stopping the sales of counterfeits by the Merchants on its platform. Jack Ma, CEO of Alibaba, has had to change strategy over the years: from denying the issue to accepting it and agreeing to cooperate with the authorities. Companies that neglect the risk of brand association in high-visibility and high-speed digital contexts do it at their own risk.

When dealing with *suppliers* the challenge is often achieving deeper technological integration. GE spent billions of dollars to develop the Predix platform. As articulated by several senior executives at the firm:

Table 3 Problems and challenges in managing different partners

		Partners' contribution in helping the digital diversifier compete in the new market	
		Limited or in a few areas	**Significant and in many areas**
Partners' Contribution in offering data in context to the diversifier	*Data that is marginal or peripheral to the diversifier's value proposition in the new market*	Q1. *Satellites* Power asymmetries among partners might lead to oversights and perception of lack of reciprocity. E.g., Apple facing the Alliance for App Fairness.	Q2. *Complementors* Brand association with partners carries high reputational risks. E.g., Alibaba association with TMall's Merchants selling counterfeits.
	Data that is of key essence to the diversifier's value proposition in the new market	Q3. *Suppliers* Seamless technological integration is key not only to enable these partnerships but also to keep trust among partners. E.g., GE's Predix alienating their partners because of weaknesses in their platform.	Q4. *Strategic partners* The contractual complexity increases exponentially to include chapters on data usage, privacy, and cybersecurity. Ex ante strategic alignment becomes even more important than in the past. E.g., Google and Apple's struggle to sign strategic partnership with car manufacturers.

> Predix had the potential to build a multibillion market for companies and as a result, partners (strategy advisors, software integrators, software houses, hardware companies, etc) literally jumped at us. Yet, we quickly started receiving complaints from our ecosystem partners because our platform was not delivering. For instance, our APIs and microservices were not enabling access to reliable data about the GE assets. And, if partners do not have reliable data, how can they go and build optimization services? Our technological weaknesses quickly triggered a break of trust, too.

Despite billions spent in development, the Predix platform had to be paused for several weeks because it could not support its partners efficiently.

On the face of it, partner integration in the digital context appears easier, quicker, and less costly than it was twenty years ago. For example, when CBRE was asked by a major retailer to improve the experience of its employees in using their offices across the globe, CBRE deployed their proprietary tenant experience platform called CBRE Host that elevates the workplace experience by blending technology and real estate and by partnering with service providers from a multitude of industries from tech through transportation to food and beverage. According to a senior executive at CBRE: "Because partnerships are now API to API, connecting companies is not too complex."

However, building these technological capabilities is much harder (and more expensive) than some people assume. The same senior CBRE executive that enthusiastically spoke about the easiness of creating partnerships in the digital context added a note of caution: "Technological integration is much more than developing APIs or doing API to API integration." As the Director of Industry Strategy at Oracle, Swapan Ghosh, told us: "It is integrating APIs with the company technology architecture which makes the real difference, and this is complex and expensive." This is an area that the big platform companies have an advantage. The Global IoT go to market leader at Vodafone commented: ". . . The digital context provides a distinct advantage to companies that have built the technological capability to integrate external partners. For example, platform businesses and born-digital companies have a clear advantage here. The likes of Google and AWS can integrate with pretty much everything . . ."

When dealing with *strategic partners*, the key challenge is mostly contractual. The contractual complexity is evident in the attempts of Amazon, Apple, and Google to enter the mobility industry. They are trying to do so by building strategic partnerships with legacy car manufacturers. Yet, data ownership, privacy, and brand/branding clauses in these strategic partnership contracts have proven difficult to overcome, and most partnerships have not gone beyond the press release stage. The problem is that writing and enforcing strategic partnership contracts in the digital context is much more difficult than people assume. For example, a senior executive at CBRE told us: "In the past, the conversation among partners would be about trust and revenue sharing. Now there are many more layers: brand, data, data usage, cybersecurity, etc. It is becoming quite complex. The legal implications are quite broad and unchartered." Given the plethora of issues to consider, it is impossible to write a contract that takes all possible permutations into account. As a result, problems will inevitably arise. For example, consider the Netflix/AWS partnership that turned sour. When Netflix entered the TV and movie streaming market, they did so with AWS as a strategic partner. Over time, AWS developed the knowledge to read and analyze content consumption data, and in 2016 Amazon launched its own streaming service, Amazon Prime. Consider, also, the experience of Vodafone. In its efforts to create a pet tracker service, the company spent two years negotiating with a large pet food manufacturer to do this in partnership. In the end, nothing came out of it. One reason was the complexity of the contractual deal: Who would own the data? Who could use the data? Whose brand would be customer-facing? Who would invoice and receive the initial payments? And so on. Another reason had to do with the lack of strategic alignment between the two partners: for Vodafone, the pet service was necessary to drive sales of its core services/devices and needed results quickly, whereas for their partner, it was an initial attempt at something "nice to have," which was a longer-term strategic option. For such complex partnerships, contract negotiations break down if there is no strategic alignment among partners – just like in the pre-digital era.

2.4 New Management Capabilities Needed for Managing Ecosystem Partnerships

Digital ecosystems help digital diversifiers enter and compete in entirely new markets but create problems of their own. Given the plethora and diversity of partners available, firms can collaborate with an array of companies, not all of which contribute equally to the relationship. This implies that the diversifier must first understand what types of partners it is building relationships with and then develop customized strategies for each. To make matters worse, the digital context has made the management of these partnerships even more complex and challenging than those in the pre-digital era. The additional challenges created by the digital context highlight the need to broaden and elevate partnership management capabilities in all firms. The skills that worked well in a pre-digital world may not be sufficient in the new context.

3 New Market Entry Strategies in the Digital Age

Having the capabilities to exploit data – the new asset made possible by the digital revolution – and then developing and implementing customized strategies to work harmoniously with the many and diverse ecosystem partners that a diversifier needs to compete effectively in new markets are key ingredients for success. However, they are not enough. Past academic research has identified numerous other factors that impact success in diversification, especially unrelated diversification (e.g., Collis and Montgomery, 2008; Gary, 2005; Grant, 2021; Kenny, 2009; Markides, 1997; Markides and Williamson, 1994; Ng, 2007; Very, 1993). One of these factors has to do with the strategy that a diversifier employs to enter a new market. Specifically, we know that the odds of success are greatly improved if a differentiated strategy or business model is employed (Geroski, 1991; Porter, 2008). This implies that the diversifying firm must not only decide how exactly it should exploit data in its possession or how it should manage its relationships with various ecosystem partners. It must also put everything together into a self-reinforcing system of activities to develop an innovative strategy that allows it to enter the new market without attacking the established players head-on. This is not an easy task.

In this section, we propose that the digital context has led to the emergence of several new business models – such as the platform business model and the business model of anything as a service XaaS – that have, in turn, given firms more choice on how to attack established competitors in new markets in a differentiated way. This has improved the odds of success because it allows new entrants to avoid head-on competition with formidable incumbents. However, given the importance of data as the asset that digital diversifiers are primarily exploiting, and given that digital technologies are now allowing companies to reach many more customers more quickly and at much lower cost, we propose that one of the new business models of the digital era is particularly appropriate for digital diversification. This is the business model of personalization at scale. We will explain exactly what this is and finish the section with a proposition: personalization at scale is a business model that requires specific capabilities to be implemented successfully. Since these capabilities are not distributed evenly among firms, this implies that unrelated diversification may not be equally attractive to all firms. We should therefore see some firms – those possessing the requisite capabilities – diversifying a lot, but many others – those missing these capabilities – would be refraining from any diversification.

3.1 Unrelated Diversifiers Need to Avoid Head-on Competition

One of the many insights that have emerged from the academic literature on diversification over the past forty years has to do with the strategy that a firm should utilize to improve the odds of success of entry in a new market. It is now generally accepted that the probability of entering a new market successfully is higher if the new entrant adopts a strategy that allows it to avoid attacking the established players in that (new) market head-on (Christensen, 1997; Geroski, 1991; Porter, 2008). For example, Michael Porter (2008: 514) proposed that "... the cardinal rule in offensive strategy is not to attack head-on with an imitative strategy, regardless of the challenger's resources or staying power." Similarly, Kim and Mauborgne (2014: 4) argued that "The only way to beat the competition is to stop trying to beat the competition." And Christensen's theory of disruptive innovation (1997) is based on the premise that to establish a foothold in a new market, entrants need to play the odds and *avoid head-on* competition with better-resourced incumbents. Examples of companies that support this proposition include IKEA, Canon, Amazon, EasyJet, Enterprise, Netflix, and Skype, among many others.

The rationale for this becomes apparent when we consider the academic findings on the track record of companies that attempted entry into new markets (e.g., Audretsch, 1995; Geroski, 1991, 1995). One of these findings is that most new entrants fail within a short period of entry. For example, Geroski (1991) reported that about 5–10 percent of new entrants fail within a year of entry, 20–30 percent fail within two years, and about 50 percent fail within five years of entry. Similarly, Dunne, Roberts, and Samuelson (1989) found that 64 percent of their sample of new US firms had exited within five years of entry while a full 79 percent had stopped trading ten years after entry. The failure rate of new entrants is so high that the new entry process has been compared to using a revolving door – new entrants are like people going through a revolving door, exiting the room as soon as they enter it (Audretsch, 1995).

A second finding from this literature is that most entrants imitate the strategies of the incumbents in the new markets they enter. For example, Geroski (1991) estimated that imitative entry accounts for 90 percent of all entry, with only 10 percent of new entrants adopting innovative strategies. It is not surprising, therefore, that most new entrants fail or that it takes a long time for the profitability of new entrants to be equal to that of the established players (Biggadike, 1979).

The high failure rate of new entrants is a reflection of the fact that when they enter a new market, they have to fight it out with incumbents in that market who enjoy first-mover advantages. Unless the new entrants utilize an innovative strategy to attack, their chances of success are limited. Since we know that 90 percent of all entrants use imitative entry to attack, the high failure rate is not a surprise (Geroski, 1991: 230). This implies that the probability of success in entering a new market is increased if the entrant adopts an innovative strategy.

Even though these insights were developed in the pre-digital era, there is no reason to believe that they are not equally applicable in the digital era. Several high-profile digital examples support this argument. For example, in 1999 Amazon launched an auction site to compete with eBay. It failed because its strategy tried to duplicate eBay and its successful strategy (Kim and Mauborgne, 2011). Similarly, Google has withdrawn from many markets where they could not offer products or services different enough to avoid head-on competition. Google +, Google Wallet Card, and Google News and Weather are just some examples on a very long list of failed ventures. Microsoft had an equally miserable experience when it tried to diversify into the search business, attacking Google. The following quote from a May 2009 Forbes.com article captures the essence of the argument well (Barret, 2009):

> *For several years now, Microsoft has spent hundreds of millions (and likely close to billions) trying to out-do Google at search. Now, the folks in Redmond have something new up their pale blue Oxfords. Microsoft is debuting a search engine, code-named "Kumo." Chief executive Steve Ballmer is likely to show it off at a conference next week. If it's anything like Google, no one will care. There are lots of good-enough search alternatives out there. Yahoo! ranks second with 20% market share. Little Ask.com is still eeking out a meagre 3.8% share. Would-be Google killers have come and gone … These rivals' strategies seem to be: Search is a big market so all we need is just a sliver to make a nice business. So they aim to be just a little different … To unseat Google, Microsoft has to be sly. Building a "more robust search experience" won't do. Microsoft will have to shock and awe. This might be about rethinking where we do our searching or how we come up with search queries …*

All these examples show that the need to enter a new market on the back of a differentiated business model is as relevant in the digital era as it was forty years ago. What is new in the digital context is *the increased number and wider variety* of strategies or business models that companies can utilize to enter new markets. This is where the digital context has made a difference.

3.2 The Digital Context Has Led to the Emergence of New Business Models

A business model has been defined as a system of interrelated activities that a firm puts together to execute its high-level strategy (Afuah, 2003; Amit and Zott, 2020; Zott and Amit, 2010; Zott, Amit, and Massa, 2011). These activities can be grouped into three main categories: *who* to target as customers, *what* products and services to offer these customers, and *how* to serve these customers, that is, what value chain activities to put in place to allow the firm to deliver value to customers (Abell, 1980; Markides, 2008).

Business model *innovation* has been defined as the discovery of a new Who-What-How *combination* in an industry (Markides, 2023). To qualify as a new business model, it has to be more than just new to a firm – it has to be new to the world or new to the industry. Similarly, it has to be more than the discovery of new activities that make up the system. As Teece (2010) suggested, to qualify as a new business model, it will have to be a new *architecture* that links the various activities of the system together. In this sense, we can have a new business model even if none of the existing activities in the system change – it can be a system that combines either the existing activities or a set of different activities in a new way (Markides, 2023).

The business model concept became very popular in the last twenty years, yet the emergence of new business models is not a new phenomenon. IKEA introduced a new business model in the retailing business in the 1950s and Nucor did the same in the steel business in the 1960s as did Dell in the personal computer industry in the 1970s. However, the emergence of digital technologies has had a profound effect on how business model choices are made and how they are implemented. At its most basic, the digital context has led to a significant increase in the *number* of viable options available for each activity in the system and that, in turn, has led to an increase in the number of *combinations* these activities can create when they are put together. Put another way, digital technologies have led to a proliferation of viable business models or strategies available to any given firm (Lanzolla and Markides, 2021; Menz et al., 2021). Whereas in the pre-digital era, a firm could have the choice of a limited number of viable strategies to choose from, the digital era has expanded the number (and variety) of viable choices enormously.

This simple fact alone has enormous implications for Strategy – for example, potential entrants now have a wealth of strategic options to attack incumbents, increasing their probability of success. Similarly, new sources of competitive advantage have been created – a firm can now enjoy a competitive advantage that is not based on its position in an industry or the strength of its internal resources but it's based instead on the business model it has developed and "how it plays the game" in its industry (Lanzolla and Markides, 2021). The proliferation of business models has also affected how value is created and distributed in a given industry and has led to the erosion of traditional sources of competitive advantage. There are other implications that flow from the simple fact that digital technologies have led to a proliferation of viable strategies and business models in any given industry, but for the purposes of this manuscript, we will focus on what this means for digital diversifiers.

For a firm considering diversifying into a new market, the availability of many more business models to choose from increases the probability that the firm will avoid head-on competition with established incumbents. This, in turn, improves the probability of successfully diversifying into new markets, something that encourages companies to undertake investments that even twenty years ago would have been considered unattractive.

Perhaps the most obvious new business model of the digital era is the platform business model (Cusumano et al., 2019; Marshall et al., 2015). Several companies, both de novo entrants, such as Uber and Airbnb, and diversifying established companies, such as Apple and Axel Springer, have utilized it to enter new markets successfully. A classic example is Apple's successful entry into the mobile phone market. In 2007, Apple was a computer manufacturer when it decided to enter the mobile phone market, in the process attacking huge competitors such as Nokia, Samsung, and Motorola. It looked like an uneven battle but the fight was short-lived – by 2015, the iPhone accounted for almost all of the profits in the industry (Marshall et al., 2015). A big reason for its success was its application store – a platform that connected app developers with iPhone users. By exploiting the power of the platform strategy and in the process leveraging network effects, Apple was able to neutralize the incumbents' huge first-mover advantages which included massive scale, huge R&D budgets, and trusted brands.

A similar example is the German media company Axel Springer. As part of its digital transformation strategy, the company has moved into the online classified job and real estate markets through portals such as StepStone Group, AVIV Group, and Immonet. These platforms have helped Axel Springer become a market leader in the job and real estate markets in a number of European markets. Other companies that have used the platform strategy to attack bigger competitors in established industries include Amazon in book selling, Airbnb in short- and long-term accommodation, Ebay in retailing, Tinder in dating, Etsy in retailing of handmade or vintage items, and Uber in taxis.

3.3 The Strategy of Personalization at Scale

While it should be obvious that aspiring diversifiers now have a number of potentially attractive business models to exploit in entering new markets, there is one business model that seems perfectly suited to leverage and exploit the new realities of the digital age – such as the availability of data, the drastically reduced costs of searching, analyzing, storing, and sharing information and the ease and speed with which huge number of people could now be reached and served, wherever in the world they may be located (Foss, 2005). This is the business model of personalization at scale, a model that allows for the provision of personalized products or services at volume and at mass market prices (Arora et al., 2008). As its name suggests, this is a business model that can offer differentiation and low cost at the same time, something that, as Porter (1980) suggested long time ago, is particularly difficult to pull off.

A good example of this is provided by GE's Predix unit (Lal, Rajiv, and Johnson, 2017; Weber, 2017). This was created by GE to provide tailored and personalized services to its clients in an effort to achieve the goal set by the then CEO Jeff Immelt of making GE a top ten software company within ten years. According to one of the senior executives who was part of this effort: *"Predix as a strategy was brilliant: to make the GE assets installed around the world (worth trillions of dollars) more productive through bespoke predictive maintenance and optimization services … what was not to like in it?"* The effort eventually failed, but the strategy underpinning it was clear – offer personalized services at affordable prices. In a similar vein, Vodafone has spent years to develop a pet tracker service which, through cellular tracking of pets, could develop personalized services for pet owners, including daily activity-based food plans. And Alix Partners, the consulting firm, has developed a database of cases that allow for personalized diagnostics of their clients.

Another example is provided by Netflix when it moved from content streaming into content production (Allen et al., 2014; Amatriain, 2013; Gibbons, 2019; Hadida et al., 2021; Richin, 2022; Taylor, 2013). There are many legacy companies that are in content production, yet most of them are struggling to respond to Netflix. What gives Netflix a competitive advantage over legacy companies such as the BBC or Disney is the fact that Netflix has the customer data and the geographic footprint that allows it to produce and deliver content in ways that existing content providers cannot match. Collecting and clustering viewing data has allowed Netflix to infer viewers' tastes and preferences. As their co-founder Reed Hastings told *Forbes* (Chmielewski, 2020): *"We fundamentally want to be better at creating stories people want to talk about and watch than any of our competitors."* More importantly, once it develops movies based on these insights, it has the footprint to distribute these movies on a global scale. As the CEO of Netflix Ted Sarandos told investors in April 2020 (Berman, 2020): *"One thing that's not widely understood is that we work really far out relative to the industry, because we launch all our shows, all episodes, at once. And we're working far out all over the world."*

Ping An in China offers another compelling example (Yu et al., 2020). By pioneering the "Internet + AI + 1,000 in-house physicians" service model, Ping An Good Doctor collaborates with offline pharmacies and hospitals to provide users with 24/7, one-stop medical healthcare services. This approach aims to address diverse and personalized healthcare needs, deliver authentic medical care, and build user trust. Building on this foundation, Ping An Good Doctor introduced an innovative strategic product, Private Doctor of Ping An Good Doctor, in August 2019, forming partnerships with twenty-nine global industry leaders. This service offers users personalized, one-on-one online consultations, round-the-clock medical support, and additional features such as an e-health profile and a tailored healthcare management plan. Doctors can monitor users' health over the long term, fostering trust and closer relationships. Through these strengthened connections, users benefit from more precise, consistent, and personalized healthcare services.

Another example is Tesla's entry in the auto insurance industry (Mullaney, 2022; Orsoni, 2022; Zarifis, 2020; Zawacki, 2021). Legacy insurance companies do not understand how to price risk for autonomous cars. This results in premiums that would be unsustainable for customers. In 2019, Tesla launched its own insurance program, starting with availability in California, where the automaker claims up to 30 percent cheaper premiums than the competition because of its ability to nail down precisely the risk profile of every and each driver. Finally, Apple is utilizing this strategy in its efforts to enter the healthcare industry (Balasubramanian, 2022; Farr, 2020; Gurman, 2022; Nellis, 2022; Samanta, 2021). Apple is building a business model that revolves around (hyper) personalized and always-available advice to people about their health. This is a business model significantly different from the asynchronous and based-on-averages approach more common in legacy national health systems.

3.4 The Underlying Capabilities Needed

Personalization at scale allows new entrants to differentiate themselves relative to the legacy incumbents, something that enhances their chances for success. It is a strategy that – unsurprisingly – became popular at the beginning of the twenty-first century, with the advent of digital technologies (Piller, 2004). This is not surprising because the successful implementation of this strategy is dependent on the three organizational capabilities identified in the previous section, all three being derivatives of the digital context: the capability to collect flows of data in context; the capability to derive value-creating insights out of this data through the fusion of AI and domain expertise; and the capability to develop customized partner strategies for the many and diverse partners in the firm's ecosystem.

The three capabilities identified here represent a significant departure from earlier frameworks about personalization at scale. While in the past the hurdles in implementing personalization at scale were mostly linked to operational flexibility and logistics (Arora et al., 2008; Zipkin, 2001), our discussion here suggests that the key to successful implementation of personalization at scale in a digital context is the capability to integrate knowledge and technology quickly and efficiently. Data, AI and ecosystems allow firms to overcome most of the legacy operational trade-offs, but these potential benefits remain untapped without the appropriate capabilities. It is perhaps not surprising that most of the successful cases of personalization at scale have been implemented by technology companies. Another way of saying this is that only a subset of companies will possess the capabilities needed for adopting the strategy of personalization at scale – and these are likely to be the firms "born digital," such as Amazon, Google, Alibaba, and Meta. These are the firms that will diversify the most by exploiting this strategy. By contrast, most other firms that do not possess the requisite capabilities will refrain from diversification altogether. The empirical evidence on diversification in the last twenty years shown in Section 1 seems to support this assertion.

The ability to execute strategies of personalization at scale does not imply that customers will be willing to adopt *any* personalized products/services. Other researchers (Kumar et al., 2019) found that artificial intelligence is aiding personalized engagement marketing and they proposed that consumers are ready for (Kumar et al., 2019): *"a new journey in which AI is a tool for endless options and information that are narrowed and curated in a personalized way."* While this seems to be the trend, the pace at which – and the extent to which – personalization at scale strategies might be appealing for potential customers is perhaps an empirical question. What is obvious is that customers make several trade-offs when considering adoption of such products and services. Trade-offs include the extent to which they are willing to trade on their privacy to get more personal service/product and the extent to which personalized products add to their self-worth vs. impacting their external/social projects. Nevertheless, when designed and executed right, personalization at scale strategies offer a formidable way to enter new markets without facing head-to-head competition.

Finally, a note of caution. The fact that digital technology has allowed for the emergence of the strategy of personalization at scale does not mean that all personalized services will be valued by clients to such an extent that a sizeable market will be created. On the one hand, consumers and industrial companies make trade-offs between privacy and personalized services and what they finally decide will be contingent on several factors, both cultural and economic. On the other hand, the market for a given personalized service might simply not be big enough to pay for the cost of delivering on the strategy. The case of Sky UK refraining from entering the market for personalized weather forecasts is just one of several examples. Overall, any considerations on adopting the strategy of personalization at scale to diversify into a new market should build on realistic assumptions on the market attractiveness and market size of the personalized service being considered.

4 The Role of the Corporate Center in Digital Diversifiers

Traditionally, the corporate centers of diversified firms had to perform three primary roles: to operate an internal capital market so as to allocate resources efficiently among the various businesses of the firm (Williamson, 1975); to coordinate business units so as to exploit any synergies and achieve overall cohesiveness for the firm (Grant, 1991); and to monitor and evaluate business unit performance (Campbell et al., 1994). The digital context has not changed these roles but has created a few *new* ones – such as the governance of customer data and the management of risks associated with AI-decision-making and the need to work with a diverse set of ecosystem partners. In this section, we will explore what these changes imply for the organization of the corporate center in diversified firms.

4.1 New Challenges for the Corporate Center

The digital context has brought to the fore *new problems* that the diversified firm needs to worry about as it attempts to manage its units. Four such problems are particularly strategic in nature: (i) customer data governance, especially now that customer data is increasingly being leveraged for diversification and is also increasingly being shared outside the boundaries of the firm with ecosystem partners; (ii) the appropriate use of AI in making decisions, ensuring that final critical decisions are always made by human beings, despite the technological superiority of AI; (iii) managing the risks that emerge by having multiple and different ecosystem partners to work with; and (iv) identifying mechanisms to ignite and scale network effects by leveraging business units that are operationally independent.

4.1.1 Data Governance

As already pointed out, data is the main asset that is being leveraged by digital diversifiers. This implies that a comprehensive data governance framework – the collection of policies, procedures, and standards that govern data collection, storage, processing, and sharing – is essential for protecting and enhancing the operational value of such asset while ensuring compliance with relevant regulations such as the General Data Protection Regulation (GDPR) and the California Consumer Privacy Act (CCPA).

Third-party data is often protected by regulation which prescribes the adoption of stringent security and privacy measures – for example, encryption techniques, secure access controls, regular security audits to protect data from unauthorized access and breaches, and data anonymization and pseudonymization. Failure to comply often has serious consequences for companies and we do have several cases of companies that have been investigated and fined under the General Data Protection Regulation (GDPR) for various violations related to data privacy and protection. For example, in 2023, Meta was fined €1.2 billion by the Irish Data Protection Commission (DPC) for transferring data of EU users to the United States, violating GDPR's international transfer guidelines. Additionally, Meta received a €390 million fine for changing the legal basis of data processing without sufficient transparency and user consent (https://secureprivacy.ai/). Another example is the case of TikTok that in 2023 was fined €345 million by the Irish DPC for processing children's personal data without proper consent and failing to secure accounts of users under thirteen by default. This highlighted significant lapses in child protection measures on the platform (https://secureprivacy.ai/). More difficult to quantify but equally damaging are the reputational risks related to such infringements.

On the operational side, data governance is aimed at ensuring data integrity, relevance, and timeliness, as well as interoperability. Given that data is increasingly shared with ecosystem partners, data governance frameworks should also include policies that outline the terms of data usage, security requirements, and compliance obligations for all parties involved. It follows that for digital diversifiers, the corporate HQ has to organize not only to ensure compliance but also to enable data integrity and interoperability, something that would be difficult without a strong and active corporate center. It follows from these considerations that digital diversifiers should build and maintain shared technology platforms and strong data governance frameworks that can be used across multiple business units.

4.1.2 AI Decision-Making

The widespread adoption of AI by digital diversifiers is not without its drawbacks. One of the concerns is the unintended harm that AI can cause, particularly for vulnerable stakeholders. These practices raise ethical concerns about the balance between efficiency and the well-being of workers (Kellogg et al., 2020; Rahman, 2021; Zuboff, 2019). For instance, AI has been used for unprecedented managerial control, worker surveillance, and optimization, sometimes with harmful consequences. In some cases, workers may adapt to or even subvert these AI-enabled systems, reflecting a growing tension between control and resistance in the workplace (Cameron, 2022; Newlands, 2021).

The adoption of AI systems can perpetuate existing biases, including racial and gender biases, which are difficult to address due to the opacity of AI decision-making processes (Bender et al., 2021; Pasquale, 2019). The increasing reliance on AI for tasks requiring critical judgments may lead to an erosion of human decision-making capabilities, as individuals begin to doubt their own judgment in favor of machine-driven decisions (Lebovitz et al., 2022). AI also poses risks related to bias and discrimination. Finally, the environmental and sustainability costs of AI are significant concerns. The development and deployment of AI involves substantial energy consumption and data processing, which have long-term implications for environmental sustainability (Sadowski, 2020).

These concerns underscore that mitigating risks associated with AI decision-making is crucial for organizations seeking to leverage artificial intelligence effectively while minimizing potential adverse effects. As is the case with data, AI is subject to regulation. The European Union's AI Act (2024) focuses on risk-based categorization and transparency while the AI Risk Management Framework in the United States (AI RMF, 2023) was released as a voluntary set of guidelines designed to help organizations manage risks associated with artificial intelligence systems. Overall, AI regulations are still in their infancy, and this institutional void creates challenges – and opportunities – which require a clear framework to be tackled.

Operationally, to manage AI risks successfully, companies should equip themselves with solid frameworks that would allow them to de-risk AI decision-making. Lanzolla, Pagani and Tucci (2024) summarized some relevant dimensions of the problem that should be managed. First, Type of AI System: A crucial distinction exists between autonomous/static systems and self-improving systems. Autonomous/static systems function with fixed parameters, whereas self-improving systems, such as deep learning models, continuously learn and adapt. The latter category of systems presents unique challenges due to their ever-changing nature. Second, Nature of Mistakes: AI errors can manifest in both pre-deployment and post-deployment phases. Pre-deployment errors include intentional issues, such as biased algorithms, and unintentional issues, such as incomplete training data. Post-deployment errors encompass unauthorized access (hacking) and hardware alterations affecting AI performance. Third, Scope of AI Decisions: The impact of AI decisions can vary from being confined within a specific domain to having systemic implications. Managing systemic decisions necessitates an understanding of interdependencies and the potential ripple effects across the organization. Extant literature is still nascent on how to establish such controls and this makes the role of the center in a diversified firm even more daunting. Effective AI risk management requires integrating domain expertise with AI insights, educating business experts on AI systems, and continuously monitoring AI decisions' ripple effects with prioritized alerts and clear escalation processes. In this light, the role of the corporate

HQ is to implement robust organizational controls tailored to the interpretability of AI systems and the scope of their decisions.

4.1.3 Digital Ecosystem Risks

Using digital ecosystem partners to execute strategy entails several risks, including dependency and power imbalances, reputation management, technological integration, and contractual and strategic misalignments (Lanzolla and Markides, 2022). For example, smaller partners – that we called "satellites" in Section 2 – can form coalitions to demand fairer terms, something that has the potential to disrupt established dynamics and force larger companies to renegotiate terms. The Coalition for App Fairness against Apple is a good example of this. Similarly, collaboration with partners that we called "complementors" in Section 2 has the potential to damage a firm's brand image. For example, Nespresso actively avoids digital ecosystems due to fear of unwanted brand associations, and Alibaba has faced numerous issues with counterfeit sales affecting its reputation.

Other types of risks can emerge from all types of ecosystem partners. For example, partners that we called "suppliers" in Section 2 present challenges in achieving deep technological integration, a problem illustrated by GE's Predix platform facing significant issues with API reliability. Similarly, partnerships with ecosystem partners that we called "strategic partners" in Section 2 are often associated with legal and contractual risks, including issues of data ownership, privacy, and branding. An example of this is the failed Vodafone pet tracker deal and the evolving Netflix–AWS relationship that has turned into direct competition. These risks emphasize the need for systematic frameworks for partner selection and tailored management strategies to effectively navigate the complexities of digital ecosystems.

4.1.4 Integration of Demand and Supply-Side Synergies

In addition to the need to manage the three aforementioned problems, the corporate center must also ensure that synergies between its units are fully leveraged. This responsibility has traditionally fallen to the corporate center, but the digital era introduces new types of synergies (Jacobides et al., 2023a) that may necessitate different approaches and integrating mechanisms (Jacobides et al., 2023b). As discussed earlier, for companies diversifying in the digital era, the effective management of data and network effects, both direct and indirect, can serve as a significant competitive advantage. Therefore, while pre-digital diversifiers primarily focused on optimizing supply-side synergies – such as shared technology or distribution channels – digital diversifiers must seek to exploit both supply-side and demand-side synergies. This shift underscores the evolving role of the corporate center in managing these emerging digital opportunities and challenges. The traditional focus of corporate centers was on ensuring that synergies related to common technologies, processes, or distribution channels were maximized across different business units. However, in the digital era, the corporate center's role expands to include the active management of digital synergies, particularly those arising from data and network effects. As demonstrated before in Sections 1–3, these new synergies present unique opportunities for digital diversifiers, allowing them to pursue diversification not only leveraging shared supply-side resources but also by tapping into the demand-side benefits that arise from network effects and data-driven insights (Aversa and Hueller, 2023; Harrigan, 2024; Tarzijan and Snihur, 2024). The exploitation of these dual synergies requires the definition and implementation of new integration mechanisms.

4.2 The Role of the Corporate Center in Digital Diversifiers: Making the Case for the CM-form

So far, we have discussed the new challenges that the digital environment has created for the corporate center of a diversified firm. Given these new challenges, we will now propose that compared to pre-digital diversifiers, the corporate center of digital diversifiers must assume a more active and more interventionist role in managing business units. There are three reasons why we propose this change.

First, digital diversifiers may appear like unrelated diversifiers of old, but they are not. Their separate units are connected together by a common asset – data – and, often, by the enactment of network effects, and this makes them more like related diversifiers than unrelated ones. This implies that the center must become active in managing the synergies among these "related" units, something that requires a shift in the organizational structure of the diversified firm from the M-form to the CM-form (Williamson, 1975).

Second, the types of synergies that digital diversifiers need to exploit – namely data-enabled information synergies and client-side synergies – require both a unified strategy for technology development, data management, and digital infrastructure and a more active management of such synergies themselves. This basically means that the need for exercising central control and identifying strategic directions is now of a magnitude that is much higher than before – even when compared to the need for exercising central control in related diversifiers in the pre-digital era.

Finally, the institutional vacuum around data and AI creates significant legitimacy risks for digital diversifiers. This implies that digital diversifiers must centralize controls on the use of data and AI. The need for these controls – and the associated advantages for digital diversifiers – will decrease as regulation becomes more prescriptive thus reducing the legitimacy risks.

The need for adopting the CM-form organizational structure follows directly from the literature on related diversification. Pre-digital unrelated diversifiers had adopted the multidivisional organizational structure (Chandler, 1962) and operated primarily as passive holding companies (Chandler, 1962; Rumelt, 1974; Williamson, 1975). This essentially meant that the corporate center exercised strong strategic and financial control over the divisions but did not interfere in their operating decisions, nor did it try to actively coordinate the activities of the various units – it simply operated a competitive internal capital market which, for various reasons, was assumed to be more efficient than the external capital market. In Williamson's (1975) terminology this was the M-form organizational structure which was perfectly appropriate for unrelated diversifiers. Chandler (1962) documented the rise of this organizational structure in the twentieth century, in conjunction with the rise of the diversification strategy.

Today's digital diversifiers are increasingly moving into markets that seem totally unrelated to their core businesses, so one would assume that the M-form structure might also be the most appropriate organizational arrangement for them. However, despite appearances, digital diversifiers cannot be considered unrelated diversifiers. Underpinning many of their diversification moves is at least one common asset (i.e., data) and very often a second one as well – technology and web infrastructure. For example, Amazon's online shopping operations appear to have no relationship with its operations in the streaming of movies (Amazon Prime), but contrary to appearances, this is not the case. Thanks to its dominance in online shopping, Amazon has a goldmine of data on customer behaviors that can be utilized by its advertising business. And increasingly this is the case. For example, Amazon has now started showing commercials to viewers in several countries such as the United States, Britain, Canada, and Germany. Viewers who want to opt out must pay a fee, something that has been estimated to add around $3 billion to Amazon's ad sales in 2024. Its access to customer data from its online shopping operations has helped Amazon's ads business become the world's third largest after Alphabet and Meta. Similarly, Airbnb transformed itself from a hospitality company to a travel company by adding real-world experiences to its offering. This might seem like an unrelated diversification move, but it's not. Airbnb is leveraging the same underlying technology, web infrastructure, and data flows to access users. Amazon and Airbnb are just two examples of a more general point: seemingly unrelated diversifiers are actually more related than they look.

This implies that today's seemingly unrelated diversifiers are very often related diversifiers whose units share assets that are just different from those shared by related diversifiers of the past. Granted, the relatedness stems from different assets than before, but it would be a mistake to ignore it or underestimate it. This, in turn, implies that a more appropriate organizational structure for today's digital diversifiers will be the centralized M-form structure (i.e., the CM-form structure in Williamson's (1975) terminology). This is because the CM-form structure allows the corporate center to not only exercise strong strategic and financial control over the units but, more importantly, to get involved in the operating decisions of the SBUs. This is vital because the center needs to be active in setting governance rules and in transferring skills and competences across units and in helping the units exploit interrelationships and synergies. It would be a mistake if the corporate center assumed a passive role (as conglomerates of old did), or if it gave the units total operational autonomy. Doing so will lead to dysfunctional behaviors, and the under-exploitation of the benefits of digital diversification.

Recent literature supports and complements our key tenet that the CM-form structure is the most effective way of organizing for digital diversifiers. First, extant literature argues that centralization enables more efficient exploitation of data-enabled information synergies. For example, Anjos and Fracassi (2015) showed that conglomerates that are more centralized relative to specialized firms create more value than specialized firms. Second, as discussed earlier, for digital diversifiers, client-side synergies are often the key driver of cross-divisional extra value creation (see also Mawdsley and Somaya, 2018). In this vein, Tarziján and Snihur (2024), synthesizing existing research on managing cross-selling and indirect network effects in multisided platforms (MSPs) such as Uber and Cornershop, theorize that the resulting increasing complexity requires higher levels of centralization.

4.3 A CM-form Organizational Structure That Is Different from Before

The CM-form structure that digital diversifiers need to adopt will be different from the CM-form structure that pre-digital diversifiers had adopted in two ways: (i) the degree of centralization and (ii) the types of synergies being exploited and the integration mechanisms being used to exploit these synergies.

4.3.1 Degree of Centralization

Although digital diversifiers need to exercise more central control than pre-digital diversifiers, this level of control will not be at the same level for all divisions and business units – some divisions will receive a lot of central control and some will receive much less (for reasons explained below). Thus, one issue that the corporate center needs to resolve early on, before it even decides what specific integrating mechanisms to use to exploit synergies, is how active it should be in encouraging the exploitation of synergies among the portfolio companies. Should it be like a Private Equity (PE) House that focuses on providing funding and governance to its portfolio businesses but avoids involvement in the operational affairs of the businesses and the exploitation of synergies between them; or should it be a hands-on manager that actively steers the operations of its businesses and gets involved in the exploitation of synergies? Deciding how active it ought to be will, in turn, determine the size of the corporate center – ranging from small as in a PE House to large as in a more active corporation.

There are obviously numerous factors that will influence the decision of how active the center ought to be, but two key ones are:

- How aligned are the interests between a given pair of portfolio companies? and
- The number and nature of assets being shared between each pair of portfolio companies.

The first factor is alignment of interests – in other words, is it in both units' interest to collaborate and exploit synergies? This would be determined by several other factors and contingencies. For example, if the two companies offer complementary goods, it would be in their own interests to help each other. An example of this would be Tesla cars with Tesla insurance. Tesla officials have said that they started the insurance business to solve a problem in their car business: prospective customers walking away from car sales after getting sky-high insurance quotes, based on the electric vehicles' high collision-repair costs. Cars and insurance are complementary goods – the more insurance products available for Tesla drivers, the more cars that can be sold; and the more cars sold, the more insurance products are also sold. By contrast, if two businesses are not complementary or, even worse, if they conflict with each other, then it's unlikely that they will naturally cooperate without direct intervention by the corporate center. For example, the digital business of Autotrader was operating as a separate unit adjacent to the print business for sixteen years. Throughout this period, the digital business was cannibalizing the print business and as a result, the two companies not only failed to exploit numerous synergies between them but actively fought and undermined each other. Yet another factor that will influence alignment of interests is whether the data exchange between two divisions is one-way (from A to B) or two-way (from A to B and from B to A). If it's the latter, the two businesses will recognize their interdependency and will be more likely to cooperate. In summary, several factors will influence whether the interests between A and B are aligned, and this alignment will vary from Low to High.

The second factor is the nature of assets being shared between two businesses in the portfolio. Sometimes, what is being transferred is data in context – for example, Netflix uses the viewing habits of its customers to help its production unit develop new content. Other times, it is not data in context that is being leveraged but other kinds of data. For example, in considering whether to start offering consulting services to airlines, the Met Office was thinking of leveraging its data and expertise in weather forecasting. Similarly, Thomson Reuters developed a business – originally called Reuters Market Light – that offered customized information to Indian farmers on weather conditions, crop yields, crop prices, and local agricultural news. This data was obviously valuable to the farmers, but it was not data in context. It is important for the center to recognize what type of data is being exploited – is it data in context or other customer data or any other non-customer-related data? Very often, it's not even data that is being leveraged. Canon's deployment of technology from its camera SBU in developing its photocopier business is a good example. Similarly, it was the competence of Honda's car division in building networks of dealers for its cars that was transferred to its lawn mower division to help it speed up the rate and improve the cost at which it can build an effective, specialized distribution network for its own products. In short, SBUs possess assets and competences that go beyond data, and these assets may be of value to other SBUs in the diversified corporation.

It's not only the type of asset that is being shared that is important. The characteristics of these assets are also critical. For example, if the asset being shared is customer data, is this data personal and sensitive enough, so that its loss or misuse would create serious reputational or legal problems for the firm? Similarly, if the asset being shared is knowledge about manufacturing or distribution or marketing, is this knowledge primarily tacit or is it codified in ways that allow for its easy transfer? In the same spirit, if the asset being shared is technology or technological know-how, is this cutting-edge and proprietary knowledge or is it easily purchased on the market. In summary, therefore, the type and characteristics of the assets being shared will impact how active the corporate center would want to be in encouraging the exploitation of synergies among portfolio companies.

Putting these two factors together provides us with a classification scheme for how active the corporate center ought to be in encouraging the exploitation of synergies among its portfolio businesses. This is shown in Table 4. The two dimensions of the table are the two areas just discussed: alignment of interests on the vertical axis, ranging from low to high; and the nature of the assets being shared on the horizontal axis, ranging from few and unimportant to many and strategically important. This produces the 2X2 matrix shown in Table 4.

In the upper-left quadrant (Q1), we have few and not so important assets that will be shared between two businesses that have high alignment of interests. In such a scenario, the corporate center can take a hands-off approach and allow the businesses to take the initiative in exploiting synergies between them. By contrast, in Q4, we have two businesses that have low alignment of interests between them yet have many important assets to share with each other. Since they have few incentives to exploit their synergies themselves, the center needs to get involved and take a very active and directive role in encouraging them to do so.

In the bottom-left quadrant (Q3), the two businesses have few assets to share and also have few incentives to cooperate. In such a scenario, the corporate center can act like a PE House, offering financing and governance to the businesses but leaving them alone to manage their businesses as they see fit. Finally, in the top-right quadrant (Q2), we have businesses that have lots of assets to share and lots of incentives to cooperate. The corporate center needs to develop clear parameters within which businesses can operate with autonomy and then allow its businesses to decide how to exploit synergies, subject to their actions falling within the set parameters.

This classification shows that there are different approaches that the corporate center could adopt toward its businesses and following one and the same for every division will be a mistake. The corporate center has to adopt customized approaches for each pair of businesses in its portfolio rather than a "one size fits all" approach. For example, the center may act like a PE House for businesses A and B but like a hands-on builder for businesses C and D. This approach inevitably increases the level of complexity inside the organization, but it ensures that the center follows the differentiated approach that is required for success.

This is a general point that is applicable for everything the center does with the units, not just the degree of control it exercises. In other words, in trying to decide how to organize to exploit synergies, the corporate center needs to appreciate that it cannot follow a homogeneous approach with all its divisions because different divisions will require different number (and type) of integrating mechanisms. This is because different units or SBUs have different levels of complementarity between them – for example, unit A may have a high degree of complementarity with unit B but low degree of complementarity with unit C. For example, Tesla's

Table 4 How active and involved should the corporate center be in encouraging the exploitation of synergies among its portfolio companies

		Nature of assets being shared between a given pair of businesses	
		Few and strategically unimportant	**Many and strategically important**
Alignment of interests between a given pair of businesses	*High*	Q1. The center adopts a hands-off approach.	Q2. Freedom in the frame: The center adopts a hands-off approach within clear parameters.
	Low	Q3. The center acts like a PE House	Q4. The center is very involved and directive

car division has many complementarities with Tesla's insurance division but few with Tesla's solar panel operations. Similarly, Apple's watch operations have many complementarities with the iPad and iPhone operations but fewer with Apple's ventures in healthcare. The implication of this is that the number and type of integrating mechanisms put in place to exploit synergies between A and B will be different from those that need to be put in place to exploit synergies between A and C. It would, therefore, be a big mistake if the center adopted the same mechanisms to exploit synergies for all its divisions and businesses.

This is an important point which is consistent with the work of Lawrence and Lorsch (1967) on how companies achieve integration and differentiation simultaneously. In their seminal study, they found that the number and type of integrating mechanisms that successful companies put in place depended on the volatility of the external environment: the firms in dynamic environments had to be more differentiated which meant that they also had to use more (and more elaborate) mechanisms for integration than firms operating in stable environments. In a similar vein, what we are arguing here is that the number and type of integrating mechanisms that successful diversifiers put in place will depend on the degree of complementarity between different SBUs and will vary by SBU. This point is also consistent with the work of Ghoshal and Nohria (1989), who argued that the internal structure in multi-unit organizations (such as the diversified or multinational firm) is not homogeneous throughout the organization but is systematically differentiated so as to fit the different realities faced by the different units. They argued that it is better to view a multinational firm as an *internally differentiated network* in which each headquarters-subsidiary link required a different administrative arrangement. In the same spirit, the diversified firm should be viewed as a differentiated network in which each pair of SBUs requires a different set of integrating mechanisms to be put in place.

4.3.2 New Types of Synergies and New Types of Integrating Mechanisms to Exploit These Synergies

We have already shown why digital diversifiers should adopt the CM-form structure and engage in active exploitation of synergies between their seemingly unrelated units. Now, we further argue that the way they exploit these synergies will be different from the way pre-digital diversifiers did it. In the past, supply-side synergies were exploited through the use of integrating mechanisms such as the transfer of managers across units or the use of incentives to encourage cooperation. Table 5 lists a few examples of integrating mechanisms identified in the academic literature. Similar integrating mechanisms could also be used to exploit synergies today, but as the examples of Auto Trader and Axel-Springer showed, the exploitation of demand-side synergies may require new or different integrating mechanisms to those used for supply-side synergies.

In what follows, we summarize the demand-side synergies idiosyncratic to digital diversifiers and, in parallel, we explore what new types of *integrating mechanisms can now be used to exploit these synergies.*

Table 5 List of integrative mechanisms to exploit synergies between divisions

- Same general manager running the various business units
- A strong shared vision to unite all units
- Strong shared values across divisions and units
- Common rituals, shared by all units
- Common conferences
- Transfer of people across units
- Active and credible integrators connecting the units and transferring learning and best practices
- Incentives and Initiatives that encourage cooperation
- Leaders running the units get regularly transferred across the company to run other units
- Common back office for all units
- A culture of openness and cooperation
- Strong and symbolic leadership at the top

4.3.3 Client Data Synergies

First and foremost, corporate centers can exploit client data across divisions, allowing the different divisions to offer more and better value to customers than what they could offer as independent stand-alone units. This potential can be achieved through more tailored value propositions, unique to each division, exemplified by increased personalization strategies as delineated in Section 3. Additionally, cross-selling opportunities can be optimized, for instance, via strategic product bundling and the facilitation of seamless "digital navigation" across the distinct value propositions offered by different divisions. Moreover, this approach can contribute to an increase in client lifetime value by setting higher switching costs, thus fostering increased client retention. We offer a few examples below to help clarify these points.

Consider, first, the integration between Amazon's e-commerce platform and Amazon Prime. By offering benefits such as free shipping, access to Prime Video, and exclusive deals, Amazon incentivizes customers to subscribe to Prime, thereby increasing their loyalty to the Amazon ecosystem. Furthermore, Amazon Web Services (AWS) and the e-commerce platform mutually benefit from shared insights. Businesses using AWS gain access to valuable customer behavior data, enhancing their online operations. Additionally, the integration of Alexa with Amazon's shopping platform allows customers to effortlessly reorder products and receive personalized recommendations via voice commands. This seamless integration across various divisions' services creates a unified and highly personalized customer experience, making it difficult for customers to leave the Amazon ecosystem.

Google also shows how the combination of client data from its diverse business units can enhance client retention and cross-selling. Google Search and YouTube, for instance, work together to provide personalized content recommendations based on search queries, making content discovery more relevant and engaging. The integration between Google Ads and Google Cloud enables businesses to use insights from advertising campaigns to optimize their marketing strategies. Additionally, Google Workspace integrates seamlessly with other Google services like Calendar, Drive, and Gmail, enhancing productivity and collaboration for business users. This interconnected ecosystem ensures that users benefit from a highly personalized and efficient experience, increasing their engagement and loyalty to Google's services.

4.3.4 Learning Synergies Derived from Client Behavioral Habits

Working in conjunction with client data synergies, client behavioral habit synergies refer to the cumulative benefits that divisions of a diversified corporation gain when they strategically leverage client habits from their various products and services, leading to increased customer retention and cross-selling. It is important to distinguish between client data synergies and client behavioral habit synergies to highlight that the latter occurs when the corporation systematically creates value propositions across independent business units, which cumulatively reduce the overall cognitive and emotional costs for clients when engaging with different divisions.

Apple's ecosystem demonstrates the effectiveness of client loyalty capital across its business units. Apple's devices, such as the iPhone, iPad, Mac, and Apple Watch, are designed to work seamlessly together, offering features like Handoff, AirDrop, and Continuity that allow users to switch between devices effortlessly. This tight integration extends to Apple's software and services. For instance, iCloud ensures that users' data is synced and accessible across all Apple devices, enhancing convenience and utility. Additionally, Apple Music and the App Store leverage user interaction data to offer personalized recommendations, further enriching the user experience. The cohesive and interconnected nature of Apple's ecosystem fosters brand loyalty and makes it inconvenient for users to switch to competing platforms, thereby increasing client stickiness.

Salesforce demonstrates how combining client behavioral habits across different business units and the members of its ecosystem can enhance client retention and cross-selling. Marketing Cloud and Commerce Cloud work together to enhance e-commerce experiences by using marketing campaign data to provide personalized recommendations and targeted promotions. Tableau's analytics capabilities integrate with Salesforce's other clouds to provide deep insights into business performance and customer engagement. This seamless data integration enhances customer experiences, drives the creation of habits, and increases the overall stickiness of Salesforce's solutions for businesses.

4.3.5 Network Effect Synergies

As we have discussed in other parts of this Element, cross-side network effects occur in an MSP when the value of the platform to one group of users increases as more users from another group join the platform. This effect is most often seen in digital platforms where different types of users – such as buyers and sellers, or drivers and riders – interact. As the number of users on one side of the platform grows, it attracts more users to the other side, creating a self-reinforcing cycle of growth and value enhancement for all participants. In addition to network effects that occur within a given MSP, there are also network effects that can occur across different MSPs that a firm has in its portfolio. As Tarzijan and Snihur (2024) point out, a growing number of firms are now managing several MSPs in their portfolio.

This implies that over and above the benefits of network effects within an MSP, the firm might also benefit from network effects across MSPs in its portfolio (Chang and Sokol, 2022; Jacobides, Cennamo, and Gawer, 2018). These (within an MSP and across MSPs) network effects are a powerful source of corporate advantage, as they amplify the value of a platform by leveraging the interactions between different user groups.

For digital diversifiers, managing these network effects is crucial and corporate centers play a critical role in doing this. Take, for example, a company like Uber, which operates in ride-hailing, food delivery, and freight services. The corporate center at Uber strategically integrates these services, ensuring that growth in one area benefits the others. When more users join Uber Eats, it attracts more restaurants, which in turn enhances the platform's appeal to even more users. This increase in engagement can also spill over into Uber's ride-hailing service, as more drivers are available to switch between delivering food and transporting passengers, thereby maximizing their earnings potential.

For digital diversifiers, the ability to manage and enhance these cross-side network effects across different services or regions can be the difference between thriving and merely surviving in competitive digital markets.

4.3.6 Pricing Synergies

Digital diversifiers may also benefit by developing sophisticated pricing models that consider the interdependencies between different platforms within their portfolio. By viewing their services as interconnected rather than isolated, companies can create pricing strategies that enhance the overall value of their ecosystem. One such method is the implementation of bundled pricing, where users who engage with multiple platforms within the portfolio are offered discounts or added benefits.

For instance, Amazon's Prime membership offers a single subscription that provides benefits across various Amazon services, including free shipping, streaming through Prime Video, and access to Amazon Music. This bundling not only increases the perceived value of the membership but also encourages users to utilize a broader range of Amazon's offerings, making them more likely to stay within the Amazon ecosystem. Similarly, the Apple One subscription consolidates several of the firm's services, such as iCloud, Apple Music, Apple TV+, and Apple Arcade, into one package. This strategy not only saves consumers money but also drives them to engage with more of Apple's services, thus deepening their connection to the Apple brand. Google Workspace (formerly G Suite) also follows this model by bundling productivity tools like Gmail, Google Drive, Google Meet, and Google Docs into a single subscription, a strategy particularly appealing to businesses. By offering a comprehensive suite of tools under one pricing model, Google encourages companies to rely entirely on its services for communication, collaboration, and storage, thereby increasing their commitment to the Google ecosystem.

These sophisticated pricing strategies, facilitated by a centralized corporate structure, enable firms to maximize user engagement across their platforms while enhancing the overall value proposition of their digital ecosystems.

4.3.7 From Synergies to Integration Mechanisms

The aforementioned synergies are idiosyncratic to the digital era, and digital diversifiers need to develop specific integrating mechanisms to exploit them (Jacobides et al., 2023b). In Table 6, we list the most frequently used integrating mechanisms for each type of synergy. These integrating mechanisms share several key commonalities that are essential for maximizing synergies in diversified companies. First, they heavily rely on interoperability, data consolidation, and standardization, ensuring that data is collected consistently across all business units. Second, there is a strong emphasis on cross-business unit collaboration, with teams from different units working together to validate insights and enhance overall value. Third, there is a focus on designing client journeys, bundled offerings, membership programs, and loyalty initiatives that encourage customers to engage more deeply with multiple services within the company's portfolio.

The integrating mechanisms described in Table 6 and those outlined in Table 5 approach the goal of maximizing synergies in diversified companies from different perspectives. The mechanisms in Table 5 place greater emphasis on organizational structure and cultural integration. They emphasize the need for shared leadership, cross-unit collaboration, and the avoidance of silo mentalities. Mechanisms such as appointing a common general manager, fostering strong shared values, and ensuring effective communication channels are designed to create a cohesive internal environment that supports the exploitation of synergies between divisions. These approaches are focused on aligning the organizational culture and structure to facilitate collaboration and mutual support among business units. In contrast, exploiting the synergies underpinning digital diversification (Table 6) requires the establishment of integrating mechanisms based on technological interoperability, cross-business unit validation, and the common design of client experiences.

Table 6 Different synergies, different integrating mechanisms

Type of synergy	Examples of integrating mechanisms
Client data	- Data Sharing Platforms: Centralized data lakes or shared databases for customer data integration across business units. - Data Governance Frameworks: Standardized practices for data collection, storage, and usage to facilitate effective data integration. - Unified CRM Systems: CRM systems that provide a single view of customer interactions across all units. - Business Intelligence (BI) Tools: BI tools that aggregate and analyze data from multiple sources to drive cross-unit synergies and enhance customer offerings.
Learning derived from client behavioral habits	- Seamless Product Ecosystems: Design of interoperable products and services that work together to create a cohesive user experience. - Customer Loyalty Programs: Loyalty programs that reward usage across multiple services within the ecosystem. - Single Sign-On (SSO) Systems: SSO systems allowing access to all services with one set of credentials, simplifying the user experience.
(Cross-side) Network Effects	- Bundled Offerings: Packages that combine services from multiple platforms to encourage cross-platform engagement. - Centralized Analytics Teams: Teams that analyze data across platforms to enhance cross-side network effects.

Table 6 (cont.)

Type of synergy	Examples of integrating mechanisms
Pricing optimization	- Dynamic Pricing Algorithms: AI-driven models that adjust prices based on cross-platform engagement. - Tiered Membership Programs: Membership programs offering access to a range of services, incentivizing higher engagement. - Integrated Billing Systems: Systems that consolidate charges for services across business units into a single invoice.

These sophisticated integrating mechanisms can only be effectively managed by a strong corporate center. The corporate center is critical in overseeing the centralization of data and resources, ensuring that the entire organization operates in a synchronized manner. It is also responsible for fostering cross-functional collaboration by coordinating efforts across different business units and aligning them with the company's strategic goals. Additionally, a strong corporate center ensures the interoperability of products and services, investing in the necessary infrastructure and systems to maintain a cohesive ecosystem. By managing data and pricing strategies at a central level, the corporate center can optimize customer value across the entire portfolio. Lastly, it plays a crucial role in designing and implementing incentive programs that drive cross-platform engagement, ultimately reinforcing the synergies across the business units. Without a strong corporate center, it would be difficult to achieve the level of integration necessary for success in the digital diversifiers of today.

5 Managing the Diversified Firm in the Digital Age: New Challenges

Given the size and complexity of diversified companies, managing them has always been difficult and challenging – the dismal record of conglomerates in the 1970s and the 1980s is a testament to that. The task is even more difficult now because the digital context has brought to the fore several new challenges and tensions. In Section 2 (Sections 2.3 and 2.4), we have already discussed the challenges related to managing ecosystem partnerships. In this section, we will explore three additional new challenges.

The first challenge is the need to find the right balance between a more active corporate center (which is necessary to exploit synergies between the various businesses) and more decentralized decision-making at the unit level (which is necessary given the volatility and fast-changing nature of the external environment). This is the traditional centralization vs decentralization tension that diversified and multinational companies have always had to face (Bartlett and Ghoshal, 1998), made even more pressing and difficult today by the new context. To reconcile this tension, digital diversified firms would need to develop guardrails that would make it clear to operational managers what decisions they should be taking with autonomy and what decisions they should not. Developing such clear strategic guidelines would ensure alignment with the overall corporate strategy while allowing flexibility at the business unit level. Additionally, middle managers would have to assume a pivotal role in navigating these tensions by acting as intermediaries who translate centralized strategies into actionable plans at the business unit level.

The second challenge is that of finding the right balance between leveraging AI for its speed and efficiency while ensuring that human oversight is maintained to validate AI-driven decisions, consider broader implications and make adjustments as needed. This would require the correct blending of data science with domain expertise. The goal would be to ensure that while digital tools and AI facilitate and enhance decision-making and operations, the human elements – such as judgment, ethical considerations, and a deep understanding of the business context – are not lost. Associated with this is the challenge of developing the appropriate corporate governance to tackle legitimacy risks without undermining innovation or risk-taking.

The third challenge is the need to manage the inevitable tensions that arise in a digital context as a result of increased transparency and more visibility on daily behaviors. On one hand, the increased transparency and visibility will facilitate better management, but, on the other hand, it will encourage suboptimal behaviors by individuals who might attempt to game the system. This dynamic can lead to relationships within the firm becoming more transactional and less collaborative, undermining long-term trust and commitment. Over time, such behaviors can decrease organizational resilience, as the focus shifts from sustainable growth to short-term gains, leaving the firm vulnerable to external shocks.

5.1 Managing the New Challenges

Challenge #1: Balancing more centralization for efficient exploitation of synergies between the different businesses in the portfolio with more decentralized decision-making at the business level.

As we already argued in the previous section, digital diversifiers need a more active corporate center to fully and efficiently exploit synergies between the various businesses in their portfolio. However, the need for more central control comes at the same time when more decentralized decision-making (necessary in today's volatile external context) is much more possible as a result of the introduction of digital technology in the workplace which has allowed for enhanced access to information, more real-time collaboration between people in different locations and more decentralized decision-making by individuals and teams lower down in the organizational hierarchy (Garicano, 2000; Hanelt et al., 2021; Menz et al., 2021; Schafheitle et al., 2020). How can this tension be managed, and how can the diversified firm achieve a balance between centralization and decentralization?

One possible way is to put in place boundary-setting parameters to guide decision-making (Ancona and Isaacs, 2019). This is not a new idea and the Strategy literature has already identified several parameters or guardrails that can be employed (Ancona and Isaacs, 2019; Eisenhardt and Sull, 2001; Hamel, 2011; Mankins and Garton, 2017; Stone, Deci, and Ryan, 2009). The question for us is: "are there any guardrails that are particularly suited to the digital diversifiers of today?"

Given today's fast-changing environment, a good guardrail to use will be the company's clear and clearly communicated Strategy choices in three areas – the customers it will target (and those it will not), the products and services it will offer (and the ones it will not), and the value chain activities it will utilize to compete in its markets (Ancona and Isaacs, 2019; Hamel, 2011; Markides, 2000). The idea is that employees will have autonomy to make any decisions that do not move the organization away from these Strategy choices but will not have autonomy to make decisions that deviate the company from its stated Strategy choices. In other words, employees will have autonomy to make decisions on things that improve the firm's operations but will not have autonomy to make decisions on things that will change the firm's strategic direction.

This sounds simple enough but survey after survey reports that the majority of employees do not know their organization's strategy choices (e.g., Devinney, 2013). This may be because many companies fail to make the difficult choices that strategy demands (Vermeulen, 2017) or because they fail to communicate them clearly to their employees (Northcraft and Neale, 1986). Whatever the reason, the result is that employees do not seem to know their organization's strategy or its strategic choices. This is unfortunate because without knowing the choices, it will be dangerous to give them autonomy.

A second way to manage the tension between centralization and decentralization is to change the role that middle managers play in guiding people in the organization. For example, Girod and Kralik (2021) found that self-steering teams would not deliver on their objectives if middle managers were not actively involved in guiding and supporting them. Similarly, Annosi and Lanzolla (2023) showed that higher levels of autonomy and engagement are accompanied by more governance and a leadership style from line managers which leverages normative and cognitive actions and a new social contract. In seeking to align autonomous teams to firm strategy, a key challenge for managers is acquiring information from their teams. Not surprisingly, autonomous teams are protective of their autonomy and can see attempts to collect information as an intrusion. Annosi and Lanzolla (2023) showed that line managers overcame this problem by creating a new social contract with their teams. Granted, teams value their autonomy, but they also understand that they need to build a better understanding of "what's going on" in the organization. Leveraging this need – that is, that even autonomous teams need to feel part of a bigger picture – middle managers can position themselves as brokers of both organizational connection and strategic information for teams, in exchange for the teams' benevolence in sharing information about themselves.

Challenge #2: Faster AI-enabled decision-making versus the need to keep humans in the loop: the role of augmented strategic controls and higher stakeholder engagement.

As already pointed out, digital technologies have revolutionized organizational control, enabling unprecedented levels of digitization, and datafication in managing workplace behaviors and processes. Scholars have explored how these advancements are reshaping organizations, influencing both the structure of work and the mechanisms of control (Bailey et al., 2019; Benkler, 2007; Cameron, 2022; Cameron and Rahman, 2022; Cardinal et al., 2017; Castells, 2000; Edwards, 1978; Huber, 2003; Kellogg et al., 2020; Parent-Rocheleau and

Parker, 2022; Rhymer, 2023; Thompson, 1989; Van Maanen and Barley, 1984; Zuboff, 1988, 2019).

In this context, the rise of AI within organizations has taken central stage and scholars have even coined concepts such as "algo controls" to describe the growing role of algorithms in directing and monitoring employee behavior. While algo controls can standardize processes and enhance efficiency, they come with significant risks related to employee autonomy, privacy, bias, transparency, and overall workplace culture (Kellogg, Valentine, and Christin, 2020; Lindebaum, Vesa, and den Hond, 2020; Minbaeva, 2021; Murray, Rhymer, and Sirmon, 2021; Parent-Rocheleau and Parker, 2022; Raisch and Krakowski, 2021; Tambe, Cappelli, and Yakubovich, 2019). One challenge for managers is how to balance the use of these technologies with the human aspects of work to avoid unintended negative consequences. For instance, Amazon's use of algorithmic management in its warehouses, where AI is used to monitor worker productivity in real time, exemplifies the power and pitfalls of these systems. While this approach has driven efficiency gains, it has also drawn criticism for fostering a high-pressure work environment, where workers feel under constant surveillance and where stress levels are elevated. This highlights the need for careful consideration of how such technologies impact employee well-being and organizational culture.

A second critical feature of managing in the digital context is the high visibility of employee actions and the immediate feedback loops that technologies enable. The effects of extreme transparency, where every action is visible and instantly recorded, are not always straightforward (Bernstein, 2017). For example, Roberts (2009) argued that transparency, rather than merely shedding light on behaviors, can actively reshape them – sometimes in unexpected ways. Employees aware that they are being monitored might alter their behavior to align with what they believe is expected, potentially stifling creativity or leading to superficial compliance rather than genuine engagement. Similarly, Bernstein (2012), through an in-depth study at one of the world's largest mobile phone factories in China, identified what he termed the "transparency paradox." His research revealed that while increased observability of workers might seem to enhance performance, it often led to efforts by employees to obscure their actions, thereby reducing overall productivity. This paradox underscores a key challenge in digital management: the need to balance visibility with autonomy. Bernstein's study further found that when zones of privacy were introduced, allowing workers to operate without constant oversight, their performance actually improved.

In summary, the introduction of AI and algorithmic controls is a double-edged sword. On one hand, these technologies offer powerful tools for enhancing efficiency, ensuring compliance, and optimizing processes. On the other hand, they bring new challenges that require managers to be vigilant about the broader impact on employee behavior and organizational culture. Navigating such challenges requires a significant shift in traditional corporate governance structures. Filatotchev and Lanzolla (2023) suggested a move toward an "open source" governance model, which emphasizes adaptability, inclusivity, and strategic foresight to better manage the complexities of the digital age.

Central to their approach is the idea of fostering greater stakeholder engagement and decentralizing decision-making. Unlike traditional hierarchical governance, this model involves collaboration with a wide range of stakeholders, such as employees, customers, and regulators, to create governance practices that are more responsive to the rapidly changing digital environment. This inclusive approach enables organizations to better identify and address emerging challenges and opportunities. Balancing short-term compliance with long-term legitimacy is another key recommendation. In a world where regulations are constantly evolving, organizations must not only adhere to current laws but also proactively build trust and credibility. This forward-looking approach to corporate governance allows organizations to adapt more smoothly to future regulatory changes and societal expectations.

The focus on strategic controls is also crucial in the digital context. Traditional governance often prioritized financial controls and short-term metrics, but Filatotchev and Lanzolla (2023) argued for a shift toward controls that emphasize innovation, adaptability, and the effective management of digital resources. Aligning governance with long-term strategic goals supports sustained growth and competitiveness in the digital era. Decentralizing decision-making is essential to responding to the speed and complexity of digital markets. By empowering local teams to make decisions, organizations can respond more quickly and effectively to new opportunities and challenges, while still maintaining alignment with overall strategic objectives. Building digital capabilities at the board level is another important strategy. Organizations should ensure that their leadership includes individuals with a deep understanding of digital technologies and their implications. This digital literacy at the top ensures that governance decisions are informed by the latest technological insights and are aligned with the needs of a rapidly changing environment.

Effective engagement with polycentric regulatory environments is also critical. As organizations operate across multiple jurisdictions with varying regulations, flexible governance structures are needed to navigate this complexity. This proactive regulatory engagement helps ensure compliance and supports innovation. Finally, addressing the ethical risks associated with digital transformation is paramount. Issues such as data privacy, algorithmic bias, and surveillance can pose significant risks to an organization's reputation and trust. Incorporating strong ethical guidelines into governance practices helps organizations maintain compliance with legal standards and uphold societal values.

Challenge #3: More behavioral visibility leading to more accountable management versus more visibility leading to gaming behaviors.

Behavioral visibility has become increasingly important as organizations undergo digitization, digitalization, and datafication (Albu and Flyverbom, 2016; Bernstein, 2012). This concept refers to the degree to which individuals' actions and behaviors within an organization can be observed, thanks to the widespread use of digital technologies. These technologies, through enhanced connectivity and data collection, enable the monitoring, analysis, and influence of behaviors on an unprecedented scale. The concept of behavioral visibility is rooted in earlier scholarly work on visibility and transparency in organizations. For instance, Leonardi (2014) introduced "communication visibility," which describes how social media platforms make individual communications within organizations more visible, thereby affecting knowledge sharing and innovation. Similarly, Flyverbom et al. (2016) explored the "management of visibilities" in the digital era, emphasizing how visibility is crucial for organizational control and coordination.

Behavioral visibility goes beyond merely observing actions; it also encompasses the power dynamics that arise from this increased visibility. Bernstein (2012) highlighted the "transparency paradox," where greater visibility can lead to unintended consequences such as reduced privacy and increased control over employees. Additionally, foundational theories by Goffman (1959) on self-presentation and Brighenti (2007) on visibility as a social category offer insights into how individuals manage their visibility within organizational contexts. These theories suggest that visibility is not just a passive condition but something actively managed by both individuals and organizations. Complementing these insights, more recent literature rooted in organizational behavior and information systems points to the emergence of active management of visibility by employees. In this vein, instead of fostering transparency and desired behaviors, the increased visibility can prompt some employees to engage in deceptive practices to manipulate how they are perceived by others. Consequently, top executives receive misleading feedback, which undermines the effectiveness of management in high behavioral visibility environments.

Given the tensions created by behavioral visibility – such as the potential for reduced privacy, increased control, and shifting power dynamics – management must adapt in several key ways. Scholars like Albu and Flyverbom (2016) discuss the challenges of managing visibility, emphasizing the need to balance the benefits of transparency with the protection of individual autonomy and privacy. As such, it is crucial for management to foster a culture of trust where visibility is used to support employees rather than to control them. This involves clearly communicating how data and visibility will be used and ensuring that privacy is respected. Second, insights based on the cases analyzed in this Element – in Sections 2 and 3 – suggest that management should balance transparency with autonomy by setting clear guidelines that protect employees' rights while still enabling the organization to benefit from increased visibility. This can involve establishing ethical frameworks for data use and ensuring that visibility does not undermine individual agency and lead to work-related stress.

Third, and perhaps even more crucially, behavioral visibility implies that top management too must increase consistency in the way they lead given that any inconsistencies are immediately visible to everyone in the organization, thus potentially triggering diverging behaviors. This is even more important for managers of diversified firms where the variance in contexts, businesses, and institutional environments amplifies the risk of triggering diverging behaviors. Perhaps in this vein, it might help if leaders could embrace a more inclusive, responsive style that facilitates open communication and collective problem-solving.

5.2 Do We Need New Managers?

In addition to the challenge of managing ecosystem partners discussed in Section 2, in this section, we have outlined three other challenges facing managers of diversified companies and proposed potential strategies for addressing them. But are managers truly prepared to tackle these challenges? How must leadership styles and skills adapt to effectively manage the complexities of a digitally diversified organization, especially when balancing central control with decentralized decision-making and maintaining consistency in a highly transparent environment? What new knowledge and competencies should managers prioritize to lead successfully in the digital era, and how can we equip future leaders to navigate the intricacies of AI, big data, and heightened behavioral visibility? These and related questions should be central to a renewed academic focus on (re)defining management for digital diversifiers and beyond.

6 Digital Diversification: Will History Repeat Itself?

The thesis put forward in this manuscript is made up of four components, each anchored in insights found in the diversification literature of the past twenty years.[2] Although the individual components are not new, it is their collective impact that has given rise to the main thesis of this manuscript – that the digital revolution of the last twenty years has *not* changed the economic logic for diversification, but has changed the context within which diversification now takes place; and the result of this has been that those companies that have the capabilities and foresight to exploit the new context will be able to diversify much more than was possible in the past (while those lacking the necessary capabilities will continue to refocus their activities).

The first component of our thesis is that changes in external market conditions (such as the digital revolution) play a significant role in shaping diversification strategies. This is an idea present in several diversification studies. For example, Matvos et al. (2018) explored how firms increase their scope during periods of high external capital market frictions, such as during the Great Recession, showing that diversification can serve as a strategic response to external pressures. Steen and Weaver (2017) focused on the energy sector, demonstrating how incumbents in established industries diversify into niche sectors in response to sustainability transitions, driven by both market conditions and regulatory pressures. And Wu (2013) examined how demand conditions across alternative markets impact diversification decisions in the cardiovascular medical device industry, showing that firms often diversify into new markets when faced with declining demand in their current markets. Our thesis in this manuscript builds upon this idea and provides further evidence that diversification is a response to external opportunities and pressures, including not only economic downturns, regulatory vacuums, and shifting market demands but also the emergence of new assets such as data, the arrival of radical new technologies, and the rise of the ecosystem economy.

The second component of our thesis is that to exploit the opportunities created by external changes, firms need certain capabilities. We particularly emphasized the importance of technological capabilities – such as the capability to develop and collect constant flows of data in context and to blend AI and domain expertise to generate value-creating insights out of it. Again, this idea is in line with several recent insights which highlight the pivotal role of

---

[2] We reviewed the literature published between 2003 and 2023 in journals from the *Financial Times* 50 list. Using keywords such as "diversification," "digital," "related diversification," "unrelated diversification," and their synonyms in Scopus, our search returned 60 papers, which we leverage here to complement and position our thesis.

technological resources in driving diversification. For example, Rodríguez-Duarte et al. (2007) explored the relationship between technological resources and diversification modes, finding that innovation often drives diversification decisions. Similarly, Miller (2004, 2006) demonstrated that firms with robust technological capabilities are better equipped to leverage synergies across business units, something that enhances performance. And Neffke and Henning (2013) showed that firms are more likely to diversify into industries where they can leverage existing human capital, thereby improving their chances of success.

The third component of our thesis is that the capabilities needed for successful diversification in the digital era are not distributed evenly across firms. Some firms would have them and some would not. This would imply a diverging pattern of diversification across and within industries. This prediction is in line with existing literature that shows that the impact of diversification in the digital age varies significantly across different industries, suggesting an industry-effect. For example, Wu (2013) examined the cardiovascular medical device industry and found that firms with pre-existing innovation capabilities are more likely to diversify successfully, leading to better corporate performance. Mawdsley and Somaya (2018) explored the concept of client-led diversification in the context of patent law firms, demonstrating how knowledge-based service firms diversify in response to the evolving needs of their clients. Karniouchina et al. (2023) focused on the motion picture industry, analyzing how diversification along the value chain – specifically in production and distribution activities – affects profitability. Matusik and Fitza (2012) posited that VC firms benefit from either low or high levels of diversification, while moderate levels of diversification are less beneficial, and linked this insight to the unique nature of the venture capital industry, where firms manage portfolios of investments that require different levels of attention and expertise. We built on this literature to show in Section 2 the role of three specific capabilities – that is, the ability to collect constant flows of data in context, the ability to blend AI and domain expertise, and the ability to manage digital ecosystems – as necessary enablers of digital diversification. It is therefore not surprising that industries where these capabilities are more frequently found are also where companies show a higher propensity to diversify.

A central tenet of our thesis is that the ability to redeploy resources effectively and orchestrate them in digital ecosystems is crucial in the digital age, where markets and technologies evolve at unprecedented speeds. In this vein, Sakhartov (2017, 2022) investigated how firms can optimize their diversification strategies by combining moderately related businesses to maximize resource use over time. This flexibility is particularly valuable in the digital context, where the ability to swiftly reallocate resources to new opportunities is often a key determinant of success. Helfat and Eisenhardt (2004) expanded on this by discussing the role of inter-temporal economies of scope, where firms benefit from redeploying resources between related businesses over time.

The fourth and final component of our thesis is that while capabilities are necessary for diversification, they are not sufficient for success. A diversifying firm must also put in place the appropriate structures and processes and manage its units correctly if it's to succeed with its diversification investments. We argued that in today's digital diversifiers, the necessary structures and the appropriate management of units would differ from those used in the past because the digital context has brought to the fore new problems and new risks for diversified firms – such as the governance of customer data and the management of risks associated with AI-decision-making and the need to work with a diverse set of ecosystem partners. We therefore proposed that the CM-form is the most suitable organizational structure for managing risks and enacting synergies in digital diversifiers and identified a number of new integrating mechanisms that the corporate center of digital diversifiers must now use to exploit the new types of synergies among its units. Several papers complement our arguments and shed light on the rising role of organization and governance as firms increasingly rely on intangible assets like data and intellectual property in the digital age. For example, Hoechle et al. (2012) investigated whether poor corporate governance contributes to the diversification discount, finding that introducing governance variables into models significantly reduces the discount, though it does not eliminate it entirely. Similarly, O'Brien et al. (2014) explored how capital structure influences diversification performance, showing that firms with more flexible governance structures can better leverage their resources and capabilities when diversifying.

In summary, our manuscript provides an economic rationale grounded in the existing diversification literature to explain the rise of the "new conglomerates" in the digital era (Harrigan, 2024; Kerr and Darroch, 2005; Sorkin, 2017). Of course, a similar phenomenon (i.e., aggressive and unrelated diversification) took place in the 1960s and several seemingly logical explanations were put forward to explain it – such as a stringent antitrust policy in the 1960s (Matsusaka, 1996), imperfections in the external capital market (Williamson, 1975), and the ability of conglomerates to sustain higher levels of debt because corporate diversification reduces earnings volatility (Lewellen, 1971). History shows that as external conditions changed and new government policies were implemented, these factors facilitating diversification ceased to be relevant. As a result, the diversification bonanza of the 1960s led to the refocusing wave of the 1980s when most conglomerates were forced to refocus on their core businesses (Markides, 1995). Some have even argued that it is the rise of the conglomerates in the 1960s that helped put an end to the postwar prosperity in the United States (Gilmore, 2018). It is therefore legitimate to ask: "Will history repeat itself? Are we now in the middle of a diversification bubble that will soon burst like the one in the 1960s? Or is digital diversification built on more resilient foundations?"

6.1 Will History Repeat Itself?

Whether the current diversification boom by certain (mostly technology) firms like Amazon, Google, and Apple will continue and grow in the future (or burst like it did in the 1960s) will depend primarily on how successful these early pioneers of digital diversification are with their diversification. If they are successful, then it's reasonable to expect the boom to continue, with other firms rushing in (Abrahamson and Rosenkopf, 1993; DiMaggio and Powell, 1983; Lanzolla and Suarez. 2012; Meyer and Rowan, 1977). If, on the other hand, these pioneers of digital diversification run into problems, then pressures to refocus will intensify and we are likely to see a repeat of history.

The question, therefore, that we must address is: "what will influence the success of these digital diversifying pioneers?" In this manuscript, we have emphasized the importance of one set of factors, all of them *firm-specific*. First, digital diversifiers must excel in collecting constant flows of data in context, then blending AI with domain expertise to generate value-creating insights out of this data, and finally managing a plethora of new and diverse partners within their ecosystems to succeed in the new markets they are entering. Second, they must strategically avoid direct competition with incumbents when entering new markets, often by deploying the strategy of personalization at scale. Third, they must put in place an active corporate center to exploit synergies among their units, and they must employ appropriate integrating mechanisms to leverage these synergies, especially client-side synergies. Fourth, they must apply new management priorities, including balancing centralization with autonomy, integrating AI-driven efficiencies with human oversight, and addressing the tensions that arise from increased organizational transparency – tensions that can lead to suboptimal behaviors and undermine organizational resilience.

Doing all these things and doing them in a self-reinforcing way will increase a firm's chances of success. But this is not enough. The strategic management literature has further argued that a company's ability to sustain its competitive advantage also relies on creating barriers to imitation (Porter, 1980) by internalizing resources and capabilities into structured organizations (Barney, 1991), and by establishing a web of self-reinforcing, opaque activities (Lanzolla and Markides, 2022). This means that each factor identified in this manuscript as important for success should not be viewed in isolation but as part of a broader, integrated strategy where each factor strengthens and amplifies the others. For instance, the ability to collect and analyze vast amounts of data effectively will enhance personalization at scale strategies, allowing the firm to better meet customer needs and avoid direct competition with incumbents. At the same time, an active corporate center that efficiently exploits synergies among units can enhance the firm's ability to manage diverse partnerships within its ecosystem, creating a feedback loop where data-driven insights lead to more effective partnerships, which in turn generate even more valuable data. Furthermore, balancing centralization with autonomy will enable units to operate with agility while still aligning with overarching corporate goals. These self-reinforcing dynamics would allow digital diversifiers to continuously adapt and evolve, making them more resilient and better positioned to capitalize on opportunities in digital markets. Thus, the sustainability of digital diversifiers' advantages depends on how well and how quickly they integrate these firm-specific factors to make imitation more difficult.

Although we have emphasized the importance of firm-specific factors in determining the success of digital diversifiers, there is no question that there is another set of factors, external to the firm, that also play a big role. Two external factors in particular stand out: the weakness or, in some cases, the total absence of regulatory frameworks around digital markets (e.g., Birkinshaw, 2024) leading to what academics have called an institutional void (e.g., Khanna and Palepu, 1997); and investor attitudes and expectations that have so far been positive toward diversification investments, something that has resulted in abundant capital being provided to diversifying firms (e.g., Filatotchev, Lanzolla, and Syrigos, 2025). As Sorkin (2017) commented: "... investors are seemingly willing to give these behemoths a free pass in the name of growth and innovation."

Lack of proper regulation has created an environment where "everything goes," enabling firms to experiment with new business models and markets, and often take positional advantages. Birkinshaw (2024: 1) argued that "... some [firms] have finessed regulations by identifying gaps and inconsistencies they could take advantage of, some have sidestepped regulations by arguing that those regulations do not apply to their situation, and others have nullified those rules by denying their existence altogether." For instance, Uber leveraged gaps in traditional taxi regulations to rapidly expand its ride-hailing service; Amazon capitalized on the lack of e-commerce rules to dominate online retail before regulations caught up; Jumia addressed Africa's logistical and financial service voids by building its own infrastructure and payment systems; Tencent filled China's payment infrastructure gap with WeChat Pay, embedding itself deeply in everyday transactions; and M-Pesa revolutionized financial services in

Kenya by creating mobile money solutions in the absence of widespread banking access. Needless to say that these institutional-based positional advantages are clearly dependent on changes in the regulatory environment (e.g., Lanzolla and Frankort, 2016).

Digital diversifiers have also benefited from positive investor expectations. When investors are optimistic about a firm's potential to succeed in new markets, they are more willing to provide the capital needed to finance such expansions. In this sense, positive investor attitudes act as an enabler to diversification. Filatotchev, Lanzolla and Syrigos (2025), building on a systematic study of S&P 500 companies in the period 2006–2020, showed that investors paid a premium over their peers to companies whose CEOs were signaling an orientation toward exploiting digital technology in their strategy. Higher premiums or, more broadly, broader access to financial resources might have created an environment favorable for experimenting with new business models and expanding into new markets.

This discussion suggests that whether the digital diversifiers of today will succeed with their diversification investments will depend on these internal and external sets of factors and how they evolve over time. First, will the diversifiers be successful in doing all the firm-specific things we identified earlier and will they be successful in doing them well and in protecting them from imitation? Second, will the lax regulatory environment and positive investor attitudes continue to prevail in the market or would the outside environment turn sour on digital diversifiers?

Putting these two factors together provides us with a classification scheme that helps us answer the question: "will the digital diversifiers of today be successful with their diversification investments?" This is shown in Table 7. The two dimensions of the table are the two sets of factors identified earlier: (i) will the diversifiers be successful in doing the firm-specific things discussed in this manuscript well (horizontal axis), and (ii) will the regulatory environment and investor attitudes change for the worse or will they remain supportive of diversification as they are today (vertical axis)? This produces the 2X2 matrix shown in Table 7.

In the upper-left quadrant (A), the external environment remains lax and benign but the firms fail to make good use of the firm-specific factors necessary for success. The likelihood of sustained success is uncertain and in the balance. By contrast, in the upper-right quadrant (B), the environment remains benign and the firms succeed in doing all the firm-specific things we identified earlier, as well as doing them well, and protecting them from imitation. The firms will likely be very successful with their diversification.

In the bottom-right quadrant C, the external environment changes for the worse but the firms succeed in making good use of the firm-specific factors

Table 7 Will today's digital diversifiers be successful?

		Will the diversifiers succeed in executing in a self-reinforcing way all the firm-specific things necessary for success?	
		NO	*YES*
Will the regulatory environment and investor sentiment change for the worse?	*NO*	*A. In the balance*	*B. High likelihood of success*
	YES	*D. Low likelihood of success*	*C. Moderate success*

necessary for success. In all likelihood, firms will continue to enjoy success with their diversification but not to the same extent as in quadrant B. Finally, in the bottom-left quadrant (D), the external environment changes for the worse and the firms fail to make good use of the firm-specific factors necessary for success. Digital diversifiers will most probably struggle with their diversifications and their financial results will be bad.

What does this tell us about the question of interest to us, which is: "will history repeat itself?" The future of digital diversification hinges on which of these four scenarios plays out. If the conditions described in Quadrant B prevail, the current wave of digital diversification will continue and may even accelerate, attracting new aspiring digital diversifiers. Conversely, if the conditions in Quadrant D prevail, we may see a repeat of the 1960s, where diversification strategies faced significant challenges and firms ended up de-diversifying. In either of the remaining two scenarios, the outcome remains uncertain and in the balance.

It remains to be seen which of these outcomes materializes. But rather than attempt to make a prediction or argue about the likely outcome, we believe that future research should focus on developing theory further as well as empirically testing some of the ideas and propositions made in this manuscript. For example, we have argued that digital diversification does not alter the traditional economic logic of diversification. Further research, both theoretical and empirical, might be required to test this thesis. As the context becomes more digitized and digital technologies expand their scope and depth of application, researchers may want to explore if new internal factors – beyond the ones described in this manuscript – might impact the economics of diversification, thus, for instance, changing the relationship between diversification and performance from an inverted U-shaped to an S-shaped curve, as proposed by Aversa and Hueller (2023).

Similarly, additional research is necessary to explore and test whether – as claimed in this manuscript – new types of synergies (such as client-based synergies) have emerged to supplement the traditional synergies associated with diversification. For example, Jacobides et al. (2023a) argued that ecosystem synergies will be critical for digital diversifiers. How do these synergies interact with one another? Are there optimal configurations, perhaps even self-reinforcing? Or will new tensions emerge? More broadly, will the new technologies help with managing the inevitable tensions among synergies, or will complexity undermine any advantage?

Along with economic, strategic, and organizational considerations, we also believe that research should (re)consider the role of management in the diversified firm. In this manuscript, we have brought forward some new critical managerial tensions. Additional work is needed to understand the many implications for leadership and management that modern digital diversifiers present. In summary, a lot of work remains to be done for us to develop a more comprehensive understanding of the digital diversification phenomenon. Yet, we believe that the research and ideas presented in this manuscript are a robust foundation to build upon and develop our understanding of the phenomenon further.

References

Abell, Derek F. *Defining the business: The starting point of strategic planning.* Englewood Cliffs: Prentice Hall, 1980.

Abrahamson, Eric, and Lori Rosenkopf. "Institutional and competitive bandwagons: Using mathematical modeling as a tool to explore innovation diffusion." *Academy of Management Review* 18, no. 3 (1993): 487–517.

Adner, Ron. "Ecosystem as structure: An actionable construct for strategy." *Journal of Management* 43, no. 1 (2017): 39–58.

Adner, Ron, and Peter Zemsky. "A demand-based perspective on sustainable competitive advantage." *Strategic Management Journal* 27, no. 3 (2006): 215–239.

Afuah, Allan. "Redefining firm boundaries in the face of the internet: Are firms really shrinking?" *Academy of Management Review* 28, no. 1 (2003): 34–53.

AI RMF, 2023. https://www.nist.gov/itl/ai-risk-management-framework.

Albu, Oana Brindusa, and Mikkel Flyverbom. "Organizational transparency: Conceptualizations, conditions, and consequences." *Business & Society* 55, no. 1 (2016): 1–25.

Alexy, Oliver, Gerard George, and Ammon J. Salter. "Cui bono? The selective revealing of knowledge and its implications for innovative activity." *Academy of Management Review* 38, no. 2 (2013): 270–291.

Allen, Grace, Dorothee Feils, and Holly Disbrow. "The rise and fall of Netflix: What happened and where will it go from here?" *Journal of the International Academy for Case Studies* 20, no. 1 (2014): 135.

Amatriain, Xavier. "Big & personal: Data and models behind Netflix recommendations." In *Proceedings of the 2nd international workshop on big data, streams and heterogeneous source mining: Algorithms, systems, programming models and applications*, pp. 1–6, 2013.

Amit, Raphael, and Christoph Zott. *Business model innovation strategy: Transformational concepts and tools for entrepreneurial leaders.* London: John Wiley & Sons, 2020.

Ancona, Deborah, and Kate Isaacs. "How to give your team the right amount of autonomy," *Harvard Business Review*, online edition, July 11, 2019.

Anjos, Fernando, and Cesare Fracassi. "Shopping for information? Diversification and the network of industries." *Management Science* 61, no. 1 (2015): 161–183.

Annosi, Maria Carmela, and Gianvito Lanzolla. "The evolution of line managers during agile transformation: From missionaries to priests." *California Management Review* 65, no. 4 (2023): 116–136.

Arora, Neeraj, Xavier Dreze, Anindya Ghose, et al. "Putting one-to-one marketing to work: Personalization, customization, and choice." *Marketing Letters* 19, no. 3 (2008): 305–321.

Arrow, Kenneth J. "General economic equilibrium: Purpose, analytic techniques, collective choice." *The American Economic Review* 64, no. 3 (1974): 253–272.

Arrow, Kenneth J. "Informational structure of the firm." *The American Economic Review* 75, no. 2 (1985): 303–307.

Audretsch, David B. *Innovation and industry evolution*. Cambridge: The MIT Press, 1995.

Aversa, Paolo, and Francesca Hueller. "Digital diversification." In *Research handbook on digital strategy*, pp. 18–42. London: Edward Elgar, 2023.

Bailey, David E., Paul M. Leonardi, and Stephen R. Barley. "The lure of the virtual." *Organization Science* 23, no. 5 (2012): 1485–1504.

Bailey, David E., Paul M. Leonardi, and Stephen R. Barley. "The shifting locus of work: Managing the intersection of organizational and occupational logics." *Organization Science* 30, no. 6 (2019): 1308–1336.

Balasubramanian, Sai. "Apple's latest report details its bold vision for healthcare," *Forbes*, July 25, 2022.

Baldwin, Carliss Y. "Managing the design of an undifferentiated good: Generative rules and the emergence of variety." *Research Policy* 33, no. 9 (2004): 1243–1269.

Barney, Jay. Firm resources and sustained competitive advantage. *Journal of Management* 17, no. 1 (1991): 99–120.

Barrett, Michael, Eivor Oborn, and Wanda J. Orlikowski. "Reconfiguring boundary relations: Robotic innovations in pharmacy work." *Organization Science* 23, no. 5 (2012): 1448–1466.

Barrett, William. "Microsoft: 'Bing' it on!" *Forbes*, May 28, 2009.

Bartlett, Christopher A., and Sumantra Ghoshal. *Managing across borders: The transnational solution*. Boston: Harvard Business Press, 2nd ed., 1998.

Baskerville, Richard L., Marco De Marco, and Paolo Spagnoletti. "Strategic information systems planning: A dynamic capabilities perspective." *Journal of Strategic Information Systems* 29, no. 2 (2020): 101615.

Baum, Joel A. C., and Heather A. Haveman. "Editors' comments: The future of organizational theory." *Academy of Management Review* 45, no. 2 (2020): 268–272.

Bender, Emily M., Timnit Gebru, Angelina McMillan-Major, and Shmargaret Shmitchell. "On the dangers of stochastic parrots: Can language models be too big?" In *Proceedings of the 2021 ACM conference on fairness, accountability, and transparency*, pp. 610–623, 2021.

Benkler, Yochai. *The wealth of networks: How social production transforms markets and freedom*. New Haven: Yale University Press, 2007.

Berman, Jeff. "Netflix subscriber growth, viewership soared in Q1," *M+E Connection*, April 22, 2020.

Bernstein, Ethan S. "The transparency paradox: A role for privacy in organizational learning and operational control." *Administrative Science Quarterly* 57, no. 2 (2012): 181–216.

Bernstein, Ethan S. "Making transparency transparent: The evolution of observation in management theory." *Academy of Management Annals* 11, no. 1 (2017): 217–266.

Bharadwaj, Anandhi, Omar A. El Sawy, Paul A. Pavlou, and Venkat Venkatraman. "Digital business strategy: Toward a next generation of insights." *MIS quarterly* June (2013): 471–482.

Biggadike, Ralph. *The risky business of diversification*. London: Macmillan Education UK, 1989.

Birkinshaw, Julian. "Too little, too late? How policymakers and regulators respond to the business model innovations of digital firms." *Academy of Management Perspectives* April (2024): 1–16.

Bolton, Ruth N. "A dynamic model of the duration of the customer's relationship with a continuous service provider: The role of satisfaction." *Marketing science* 17, no. 1 (1998): 45–65.

Boudreau, Kevin, Lars Bo Jeppesen, and Milan Miric. "The paradox of platform-based entrepreneurship: Competing while sharing resources." Available at *SSRN* 3897435 (2021).

Brighenti, Andrea Mubi. "Visibility: A category for the social sciences." *Current Sociology* 55, no. 3 (2007): 323–342.

Brusoni, Stefano, and Andrea Prencipe. "The organization of innovation in ecosystems: Problem framing, problem solving, and patterns of coupling." In *Collaboration and competition in business ecosystems*, pp. 167–194. Leeds: Emerald Group, 2013.

Brynjolfsson, Erik, and Andrew McAfee. *The second machine age: Work, progress, and prosperity in a time of brilliant technologies*. WW Norton, 2014.

Bughin, Jacques, Jeongmin Seong, James Manyika, Michael Chui, and Raoul Joshi. "Notes from the AI frontier: Modeling the impact of AI on the world economy." *McKinsey Global Institute* 4, no. 1 (2018): 1–64.

Cameron, Donald. "AI-enabled management control systems: Contested algorithms and worker agency." *Journal of Management Studies* 59, no. 5 (2022): 1234–1257.

Cameron, Lindsey D., and Hatim Rahman. "Expanding the locus of resistance: Understanding the co-constitution of control and resistance in the gig economy." *Organization Science* 33, no. 1 (2022): 38–58.

Campa, Jose Manuel, and Simi Kedia. "Explaining the diversification discount." *The Journal of Finance* 57, no. 4 (2002): 1731–1762.

Campbell, Andrew, Michael Goold, and Markis Alexander. *Corporate-level strategy*. John Wiley & Sons, Incorporated/Books, 1994.

Cardinal, Laura B., Markus Kreutzer, and C. Chet Miller. "An aspirational view of organizational control research: Re-invigorating empirical work to better meet the challenges of 21st century organizations." *Academy of Management Annals* 11, no. 2 (2017): 559–592.

Castells, Manuel. "Toward a sociology of the network society." *Contemporary Sociology* 29, no. 5 (2000): 693–699.

Chan, Kim, Oh Young Koo, and Renee Mauborgne. "Successes and failures of Amazon's growth strategies," INSEAD case IN1398, 2017.

Chandler, Alfred D. *Strategy and structure: Chapters in the history of the American industrial enterprise*. Cambridge, MA: MIT Press, 1962.

Chang, Hung-Hao, and D. Daniel Sokol. "How incumbents respond to competition from innovative disruptors in the sharing economy – The impact of Airbnb on hotel performance." *Strategic Management Journal* 43, no. 3 (2022): 425–446.

Chmielewski, Dawn. "How Netflix's Reed Hastings rewrote the Hollywood script," *Forbes*, September 7, 2020.

Christensen, Clayton M. *The innovator's dilemma: When new technologies cause great firms to fail*. Boston: Harvard Business Review Press, 1997.

Cohen, Susan L., and Mary Tripsas. "Managing technological transitions by building bridges." *Academy of Management Journal* 61, no. 6 (2018): 2319–2342.

Collis, David J., and Cynthia A. Montgomery. "Competing on resources." *Harvard Business Review* 86, no. 7/8 (2008): 140.

Creutzig, Felix, Daron Acemoglu, Xuemei Bai, et al. "Digitalization and the anthropocene." *Annual Review of Environment and Resources* 47, no. 1 (2022): 479–509.

Cusumano, Michael, Annabelle Gawer, and David Yoffie. *The business of platforms: Strategy in the age of digital competition, innovation and power*. New York: HarperCollins, 2019.

Devinney, Timothy. "When CEOs talk strategy, is anybody listening?" *Harvard Business Review* 91, no. 6 (2013): 28.

DiMaggio, Paul J., and Walter W. Powell. "The iron cage revisited: Institutional isomorphism and collective rationality in organizational fields." *American Sociological Review* 48, no. 2 (1983): 147–160.

Dunne, Timothy, Mark J. Roberts, and Larry Samuelson. "Firm entry and postentry performance in the US chemical industries." *The Journal of Law and Economics* 32, no. 2, Part 2 (1989): S233–S271.

Edwards, Richard C. "The social relations of production at the point of production." *Insurgent Sociologist* 8, no. 2–3 (1978): 109–125.

Eisenhardt, Kathleen M., and Donald N. Sull. *Strategy as simple rules*. Boston: Harvard Business, 2001.

Faraj, Samer, Sirkka L. Jarvenpaa, and Ann Majchrzak. "Knowledge collaboration in online communities." *Organization Science* 22, no. 5 (2011): 1224–1239.

Farr, Christina. "Apple still has a lot of room to grow in the $3.5 trillion health care sector," *CNBC*, June 20, 2020.

Filatotchev, Igor, and Gianvito Lanzolla. "'Open source corporate governance' in the era of digital transformation." In Carmelo Cennamo, Giambattista Danino and Feng Zhu (eds.) *Research Handbook on Digital Strategy*, pp. 309–323. London: Edward Elgar, 2023.

Filatotchev, Igor, Gianvito Lanzolla, and Evangelos Syrigos. "Impact of CEO's digital technology orientation and board characteristics on firm value: A signaling perspective." *Journal of Management* 51, no. 2 (2025): 875–912.

Flyverbom, Mikkel, Jens Hemmingsen, and Anne Hansen. "The transparency-visibility nexus in organizations." *Organization Studies* 37, no. 10 (2016): 1373–1390.

Foss, Nicolai J. *Strategy, economic organization, and the knowledge economy: The coordination of firms and resources*. Oxford: Oxford University Press, 2005.

Frankort, Hans T. W. "Open innovation norms and knowledge transfer in multinational corporations: Cross-level effects on discontinuous innovations." *Journal of International Business Studies* 44, no. 7 (2013): 586–613.

Garicano, Luis. "Hierarchies and the organization of knowledge in production." *Journal of Political Economy* 108, no. 5 (2000): 874–904.

Gary, Shayne. "Implementation strategy and performance outcomes in related diversification." *Strategic Management Journal* 26, no. 7 (2005): 643–664.

Geroski, Paul. *Market dynamics and entry*. Oxford: Basil Blackwell, 1991.

Geroski, Paul A. "What do we know about entry?" *International Journal of Industrial Organization* 13, no. 4 (1995): 421–440.

Ghoshal, Sumantra, and Nitin Nohria. "Internal differentiation within multinational corporations." *Strategic Management Journal* 10, no. 4 (1989): 323–337.

Gibbons, Serenity. "What the rise of Netflix's original content can teach leaders about diversity," *Forbes*, May 21, 2019.

Gilmore, Nicholas. "The forgotten history of how 1960s conglomerates derailed the American dream," *Saturday Evening Post*, November 1, 2018.

Girod, Stéphane J. G., and Martin Králik. *Resetting management: Thrive with agility in the age of uncertainty.* London: Kogan Page, 2021.

Goffman, Erving. *The presentation of self in everyday life.* New York: Anchor Books, 1959.

Grant, Robert M. "The resource-based theory of competitive advantage: Implications for strategy formulation." *California Management Review* 33, no. 3 (1991): 114–135.

Grant, Robert M. *Contemporary strategy analysis.* London: John Wiley & Sons, 2021.

Guardian. "Amazon buys US medical provider as it cements move into healthcare," *The Guardian*, July 21, 2022.

Gupta, Praveen K., and Valarie A. Zeithaml. "Marketing metrics: The definitive guide to measuring marketing performance." *Journal of Marketing* 70, no. 3 (2006): 102–104.

Gurman, Mark. "Apple argues it's now a major force in the health care world," *Bloomberg UK*, July 20, 2022.

Hadida, Allègre L., Joseph Lampel, David Walls, and Amit Joshi. "Hollywood studio filmmaking in the age of Netflix: A tale of two institutional logics." *Journal of Cultural Economics* 45 (2021): 213–238.

Hamel, Gary. "First, let's fire all the managers." *Harvard Business Review* 89 no. 12 (2011): 48–60.

Hanelt, André, René Bohnsack, David Marz, and Cláudia Antunes Marante. "A systematic review of the literature on digital transformation: Insights and implications for strategy and organizational change." *Journal of Management Studies* 58, no. 5 (2021): 1159–1197.

Harrigan, Kathryn Rudie. "Endgame in the Internet Era." *Strategic Management Review* 4, no. 2 (2023): 231–260.

Harrigan, Kathryn. "Rise of the new conglomerates." *Strategic Management Review*, in press.

Helfat, Constance E., and Kathleen M. Eisenhardt. "Inter-temporal economies of scope, organizational modularity, and the dynamics of diversification." *Strategic Management Journal* 25, no. 13 (2004): 1217–1232.

Hoechle, Daniel, Markus Schmid, Ingo Walter, and David Yermack. "How much of the diversification discount can be explained by poor corporate governance?" *Journal of Financial Economics* 103, no. 1 (2012): 41–60.

Huber, George P. *The necessary nature of future firms: Attributes of survivors in a changing world.* London: Sage, 2003.

Jacobides, Michael G. "How to compete when industries digitize and collide: An ecosystem development framework." *California Management Review* 64, no. 3 (2022): 99–123.

Jacobides, Michael G., Carmelo Cennamo, and Annabelle Gawer. "Towards a theory of ecosystems." *Strategic Management Journal* 39, no. 8 (2018): 2255–2276.

Jacobides, Michael G., Dalbert Ma, and Yuri Romanenkov. "From related diversification to internal ecosystems: Unlocking value in multi-business firms," London Business School Working Paper, 2023a.

Jacobides, Michael G., Dalbert Ma, and Yuri Romanenkov. "Setting up your HQ for success: Value from corporate design and open ecosystems," London Business School Working Paper, 2023b

Kapoor, Rahul, and Joon Mahn Lee. "Coordinating and competing in ecosystems: How organizational forms shape new technology investments." *Strategic Management Journal* 34, no. 3 (2013): 274–296.

Karniouchina, Ekaterina, Stephen J. Carson, William L. Moore, Kumar R. Sarangee, and Can Uslay. "The varying returns to diversification along the value chain." *Strategy Science* 8, no. 1 (2023): 44–61.

Kellogg, Katherine C., Melissa A. Valentine, and Angele Christin. "Algorithms at work: The new contested terrain of control." *Academy of Management Annals* 14, no. 1 (2020): 366–410.

Kenny, Graham. *Diversification strategy: How to grow a business by diversifying successfully.* London: Kogan Page, 2009.

Kerr, Gerry, and James Darroch. "Insights from the new conglomerates." *Business Horizons* 48, no. 4 (2005): 347–361.

Khanna, Tarun, and Krishna Palepu. "Why focused strategies may be wrong for emerging markets." *Harvard Business Review* 75, no. 4 (1997): 41–51.

Kim, W. Chan, and Renée Mauborgne. *Blue ocean strategy.* Boston: Harvard Business Review (2011).

Kim, W. Chan, and Renee Mauborgne. *Blue ocean strategy, expanded edition: How to create uncontested market space and make the competition irrelevant.* Boston: Harvard Business Review Press, 2014.

Koutroumpis, Pantelis, Aija Leiponen, and Llewellyn DW Thomas. "Small is big in ICT: The impact of R&D on productivity." *Telecommunications Policy* 44, no. 1 (2020): 101833.

Kumar, Vipin, Bharath Rajan, Rajkumar Venkatesan, and Jim Lecinski. "Understanding the role of artificial intelligence in personalized engagement marketing." *California Management Review* 61, no. 4 (2019): 135–155.

Kumar, Viswanathan, and Werner Reinartz. "Creating enduring customer value." *Journal of Marketing* 80, no. 6 (2016): 36–68.

Lal, Rajiv, and Scott Johnson. "GE Digital," Harvard Business School Case 517–063, February 2017.

Lanzolla, Gianvito, Margherita Pagani, and Christopher L. Tucci. "Seeking a piece of disguised hay in a haystack? How to implement organizational controls for fair and justifiable AI-enabled decisions. " Bayes Business School Working Paper, 2025.

Lanzolla, Gianvito, and Alessandro Giudici. "Pioneering strategies in the digital world: Insights from the Axel Springer case." *Business History* 59, no. 5 (2017): 744–777.

Lanzolla, Gianvito, and Constantinos Markides. "A business model view of strategy." *Journal of Management Studies* 58, no. 2 (2021): 540–553.

Lanzolla, Gianvito, and Constantinos Markides. "How to choose the right ecosystem partners for your business." *Harvard Business Review* (2022): 1–7.

Lanzolla, Gianvito, and Fernando F. Suarez. "Closing the technology adoption – use divide: The role of contiguous user bandwagon." *Journal of Management* 38, no. 3 (2012): 836–859.

Lanzolla, Gianvito, Danilo Pesce, and Christopher L. Tucci. "The digital transformation of search and recombination in the innovation function: Tensions and an integrative framework." *Journal of Product Innovation Management* 38, no. 1 (2021): 90–113.

Lanzolla, Gianvito, and Hans TW Frankort. "The online shadow of offline signals: Which sellers get contacted in online B2B marketplaces?" *Academy of Management Journal* 59, no. 1 (2016): 207–231.

Lawrence, Paul R., and Jay W. Lorsch. "Differentiation and integration in complex organizations." *Administrative Science Quarterly* June (1967): 1–47.

Lebovitz, Sarah, Hila Lifshitz-Assaf, and Natalia Levina. "To engage or not to engage with AI for critical judgments: How professionals deal with opacity when using AI for medical diagnosis." *Organization Science* 33, no. 1 (2022): 126–148.

Lee, Jaegul, and Nicholas Berente. Digital innovation and the division of innovative labor: Digital controls in the automotive industry. *Organization Science* 23, no. 5 (2012): 1428–1447.

Leonardi, Paul M. "Social media, knowledge sharing, and innovation: Toward a theory of communication visibility." *Information Systems Research* 25, no. 4 (2014): 796–816.

Leten, Bart, Wim Vanhaverbeke, Nadine Roijakkers, André Clerix, and Johan Van Helleputte. "IP models to orchestrate innovation ecosystems: IMEC, a public research institute in nano-electronics." *California Management Review* 55, no. 4 (2013): 51–64.

Lewellen, Wilbur G. "A pure financial rationale for the conglomerate merger." *The Journal of Finance* 26, no. 2 (1971): 521–537.

Lindebaum, Dirk, Mikko Vesa, and Frank Den Hond. "Insights from 'the machine stops' to better understand rational assumptions in algorithmic decision making and its implications for organizations." *Academy of Management Review* 45, no. 1 (2020): 247–263.

Mankins, Michael, and Eric Garton. "How Spotify balances employee autonomy and accountability," *Harvard Business Review,* online edition 95, no. 1, February 9, 2017.

Manral, Lalit, and Kathryn R. Harrigan. "Corporate advantage in customer-centric diversification." *Journal of Strategic Marketing* 26, no. 6 (2018a): 498–519.

Manral, Lalit, and Kathryn R. Harrigan. "The logic of demand-side diversification: Evidence from the US telecommunications sector, 1990–1996." *Journal of Business Research* 85 (2018b): 127–141.

Manyika, James. "Big data: The next frontier for innovation, competition, and productivity." *McKinsey Global Institute* 1 (2011): 1–13.

Markides, Constantinos C. "Consequences of corporate refocusing: Ex ante evidence." *Academy of Management Journal* 35, no. 2 (1992): 398–412.

Markides, Constantinos C. *Diversification, refocusing, and economic performance*. Boston: MIT Press, 1995.

Markides, Constantinos C. "To diversify or not to diversify." *Harvard Business Review* 75, no. 6 (1997): 93–186.

Markides, Constantinos C. *All the right moves: A guide to crafting breakthrough strategy*. Boston: Harvard Business Press, 2000.

Markides, Constantinos C. *Game-changing strategies: How to create new market space in established industries by breaking the rules*. San Francisco: John Wiley & Sons, 2008.

Markides, Constantinos C. *Organizing for the new normal*. London: Kogan Page, 2021.

Markides, Constantinos C. *Business model innovation: Strategic and organizational issues for established firms*. Cambridge: Cambridge University Press, 2023.

Markides, Constantinos C., and Peter J. Williamson. "Related diversification, core competences and corporate performance." *Strategic Management Journal* 15, no. S2 (1994): 149–165.

Marshall, Anthony, Stefan Mueck, and Rebecca Shockley. "How leading organizations use big data and analytics to innovate." *Strategy & Leadership* 43, no. 5 (2015): 32–39.

Matsusaka, John G. "Did tough antitrust enforcement cause the diversification of American corporations?" *Journal of Financial and Quantitative Analysis* 31, no. 2 (1996): 283–294.

Matusik, Sharon F., and Markus A. Fitza. "Diversification in the venture capital industry: Leveraging knowledge under uncertainty." *Strategic Management Journal* 33, no. 4 (2012): 407–426.

Matvos, Gregor, Amit Seru, and Rui C. Silva. "Financial market frictions and diversification." *Journal of Financial Economics* 127, no. 1 (2018): 21–50.

Mawdsley, John K., and Deepak Somaya. "Demand-side strategy, relational advantage, and partner-driven corporate scope: The case for client-led diversification." *Strategic Management Journal* 39, no. 7 (2018): 1834–1859.

Mayer-Schönberger, Viktor, and Kenneth Cukier. *Big data: A revolution that will transform how we live, work, and think.* Boston: Houghton Mifflin Harcourt, 2013.

McAfee, Andrew, and Erik Brynjolfsson. "Big Data: The Management Revolution." *Harvard Business Review* 90, no. 10 (2012): 60–68.

McKenna, Beth. "Amazon launches fitness service – Watch out Peleton!" *The Motley Fool*, September 29, 2021.

Menz, Markus, Sven Kunisch, Julian Birkinshaw, et al. "Corporate strategy and the theory of the firm in the digital age." *Journal of Management Studies* 58, no. 7 (2021): 1695–1720.

Meyer, John W., and Brian Rowan. "Institutionalized organizations: Formal structure as myth and ceremony." *American Journal of Sociology* 83, no. 2 (1977): 340–363.

Miller, Douglas J. "Firms' technological resources and the performance effects of diversification: A longitudinal study." *Strategic Management Journal* 25, no. 11 (2004): 1097–1119.

Miller, Douglas J. "Technological diversity, related diversification, and firm performance." *Strategic Management Journal* 27, no. 7 (2006): 601–619.

Minbaeva, Dana. "Disrupted HR?" *Human Resource Management Review* 31, no. 4 (2021): 100820.

Mishra, Mama and Jeffrey Dastin. "Amazon makes $5.6bn move into healthcare," *Financial Review*, July 22, 2022.

Mullaney, Tim. "Why Tesla and GM want to be big in a new kind of car insurance business," *CNBC Tech Drivers*, February 19, 2022.

Murray, Alex, J. E. N. Rhymer, and David G. Sirmon. "Humans and technology: Forms of conjoined agency in organizations." *Academy of Management Review* 46, no. 3 (2021): 552–571.

Neffke, Frank, and Martin Henning. "Skill relatedness and firm diversification." *Strategic Management Journal* 34, no. 3 (2013): 297–316.

Nellis, Stephen. "Apple outlines health technology strategy in new report," *Reuters*, July 20, 2022.

Newlands, Gemma. "Algorithmic surveillance in the gig economy: The organization of work through Lefebvrian conceived space." *Organization Studies* 42, no. 5 (2021): 719–737.

Ng, Desmond W. "A modern resource-based approach to unrelated diversification." *Journal of Management Studies* 44, no. 8 (2007): 1481–1502.

Northcraft, Gregory B., and Margaret A. Neale "Opportunity costs and the framing of resource allocation decisions." *Organizational Behavior and Human Decision Processes* 37, no. 3 (1986): 348–356.

O'Brien, Jonathan P., Parthiban David, Toru Yoshikawa, and Andrew Delios. "How capital structure influences diversification performance: A transaction cost perspective." *Strategic Management Journal* 35, no. 7 (2014): 1013–1031.

Orsoni, Damien. "How Tesla is planning to conquer the auto insurance market with its usage-based insurance programme," Ptolemus Consulting group *Insights*, May 25, 2022.

Parent-Rocheleau, Xavier, and Sharon K. Parker. "Algorithms as work designers: How algorithmic management influences the design of jobs." *Human Resource Management Review* 32, no. 3 (2022): 100838.

Pasquale, Frank. "The black box society: The secret algorithms that control money and information." *Harvard Law Review* 128, no. 4 (2019): 1202–1240.

Penrose, Edith Tilton. *The theory of the growth of the firm.* Oxford: Oxford University Press, 1959.

Piller, Frank T. "Mass customization: Reflections on the state of the concept." *International Journal of Flexible Manufacturing Systems* 16 (2004): 313–334.

Porter, Michael E. *Competitive strategy: Techniques for analyzing industries and competitors.* New York: Free Press, 1980.

Porter, Michael E. *Competitive advantage: Creating and sustaining superior performance.* London: Simon and Schuster, 2008.

Porter, Michael E., and James E. Heppelmann. "Why every organization needs an augmented reality strategy." *Harvard Business Review,* November–December (2017): 2–18.

Rahman, Arafat. "Sources and categories of well-being: A systematic review and research agenda." *Journal of Service Theory and Practice* 31, no. 1 (2021): 1–33.

Raisch, Sebastian, and Sebastian Krakowski. "Artificial intelligence and management: The automation – augmentation paradox." *Academy of Management Review* 46, no. 1 (2021): 192–210.

Rhymer, Jen. "Location-independent organizations: Designing collaboration across space and time." *Administrative Science Quarterly* 68, no. 1 (2023): 1–43.

Richin, Jose. "Will Netflix become the next blockbuster?" *California Management Review* 65, no. 1 (2022): 1–10.

Roberts, John. "No one is as invisible as you think: Some thoughts on visuality in modern organizations." *Academy of Management Annals* 3, no. 1 (2009): 1–38.

Rodríguez-Duarte, Antonio, Francesco D. Sandulli, Beatriz Minguela-Rata, and José Ignacio López-Sánchez. "The endogenous relationship between innovation and diversification, and the impact of technological resources on the form of diversification." *Research Policy* 36, no. 5 (2007): 652–664.

Rumelt, Richard P. *Strategy, structure and economic performance.* Boston: Division of Research, Harvard Business School, 1974.

Rumelt, Richard P. "Diversification strategy and profitability." *Strategic Management Journal* 3, no. 4 (1982): 359–369.

Rust, Roland T., Katherine N. Lemon, and Valarie A. Zeithaml. "Return on marketing: Using customer equity to focus marketing strategy." *Journal of Marketing* 68, no. 1 (2004): 109–127.

Sadowski, Jathan. "The internet of landlords: Digital platforms and new mechanisms of rentier capitalism." *Antipode* 52, no. 2 (2020): 562–580.

Sakhartov, Arkadiy V. "Economies of scope, resource relatedness, and the dynamics of corporate diversification." *Strategic Management Journal* 38, no. 11 (2017): 2168–2188.

Sakhartov, Arkadiy V. "Corporate diversification and risk: Portfolio effects and resource redeployability." *Strategy Science* 7, no. 4 (2022): 317–329.

Samanta, Sunny. "Why Apple is moving into health care?" *Open Growth Hub*, February 24, 2021.

Schafheitle, Simon, Antoinette Weibel, Isabel Ebert, et al. "No stone left unturned? Toward a framework for the impact of datafication technologies on organizational control." *Academy of Management Discoveries* 6, no. 3 (2020): 455–487.

Schmidt, Florian L., Madadok F. Madadok, and Mark E. Keil. "The influence of trust on project outcomes: A social exchange theory perspective." *MIS Quarterly* 40, no. 2 (2016): 507–540.

Snihur, Yuliya, and Jorge Tarzijan. "Managing complexity in a multi-business-model organization." *Long Range Planning* 51, no. 1 (2018): 50–63.

Sorkin, Andrew Ross. "Conglomerates didn't die: They look like Amazon," *The New York Times*, June 19, 2017.

Steen, Markus, and Tyson Weaver. "Incumbents' diversification and cross-sectorial energy industry dynamics." *Research Policy* 46, no. 6 (2017): 1071–1086.

Stone, Dan N., Edward L. Deci, and Richard M. Ryan "Beyond talk: Creating autonomous motivation through self-determination theory." *Journal of General Management* 34, no. 3 (2009): 75–91.

Tambe, Prasanna, Peter Cappelli, and Valery Yakubovich. "Artificial intelligence in human resources management: Challenges and a path forward." *California Management Review* 61, no. 4 (2019): 15–42.

Tarzijan, J., and Snihur, Y. "Centralization decisions in multisided platform portfolios." *Academy of Management Perspectives* (2024), (ja), pp.amp-2023.

Taylor, Frances. "Netflix to move into original movie production," *Digital Spy*, October 22, 2013.

Teece, David J. "Business models, business strategy and innovation." *Long Range Planning* 43, no. 2–3 (2010): 172–194.

Thomas, Llewellyn D. W., Aija Leiponen, and Pantelis Koutroumpis. "Markets for data." *Industrial and Corporate Change* 29, no. 3 (2020): 645–660.

Thompson, James D. *Organizations in action: Social science bases of administrative theory*. New York: McGraw-Hill, 1989.

Van Maanen, John, and Stephen R. Barley. "Occupational communities: Culture and control in organizations." *Research in Organizational Behavior* 6, (1984): 287–365.

Venkatesan, Rajkumar, and Vita Kumar. "A customer lifetime value framework for customer selection and resource allocation strategy." *Journal of Marketing* 68, no. 4 (2004): 106–125.

Vermeulen, Freek. "Many strategies fail because they are not actually strategies," *Harvard Business Review*, online edition, November 8, 2017.

Very, Philippe. "Success in diversification: Building on core competences." *Long Range Planning* 26, no. 5 (1993): 80–92.

Villalonga, Belen. "Does diversification cause the 'diversification discount'?" *Financial Management* July (2004): 5–27.

Weber, A. "GE 'Predix' the future of manufacturing." *Assembly* 60, no. 3 (2017): GE70–GE76.

Williamson, Oliver E. *Markets and hierarchies: Analysis and antitrust implications*. New York: Free Press, 1975.

Wu, Brian. "Opportunity costs, industry dynamics, and corporate diversification: Evidence from the cardiovascular medical device industry, 1976–2004." *Strategic Management Journal* 34, no. 11 (2013): 1265–1287.

Yoo, Youngjin. "Computing in everyday life: A call for research on experiential computing." *MIS Quarterly* June (2010): 213–231.

Yu, Howard, Yunfei Feng, and Anouk Lavoie Orlick. "Ping An: How a Chinese Insurance firm became a tech giant (A)," IMD case study Ref IMD-7–2138, November 2020.

Zarifis, Alex. "Why is Tesla selling insurance and what does it mean for drivers?" *The Conversation*, January 31, 2020.

Zawacki, Tim. "Latest Tesla insurance offering is more evolutionary than revolutionary," *S&P Global Market Intelligence*, January 13, 2021.

Zhu, Kevin, Kenneth L. Kraemer, and Sean Xu. "The process of innovation assimilation by firms in different countries: A technology diffusion perspective on E-business." *Management Science* 52, no. 10 (2016): 1557–1576.

Zipkin, Paul. "The limits of mass customization." *MIT Sloan Management Review* 42, no. 3 (2001): 81.

Zott, Christoph, and Raphael Amit. "Business model design: An activity system perspective." *Long Range Planning* 43, no. 2–3 (2010): 216–226.

Zott, Christoph, Raphael Amit, and Lorenzo Massa. "The business model: Theoretical roots, recent developments, and future research." *IESE Research Papers* 3, no. 4 (2010): 1–43.

Zott, Christoph, Raphael Amit, and Lorenzo Massa. "The business model: recent developments and future research." *Journal of Management* 37, no. 4 (2011): 1019–1042.

Zuboff, Shoshana. "Dilemmas of transformation in the age of the smart machine." *Pub Type* 81 (1988): 17.

Zuboff, Shoshana. *The age of surveillance capitalism.* London: Profile Books, 2019.

For EU product safety concerns, contact us at Calle de José Abascal, 56–1°,
28003 Madrid, Spain or eugpsr@cambridge.org.

www.ingramcontent.com/pod-product-compliance
Ingram Content Group UK Ltd.
Pitfield, Milton Keynes, MK11 3LW, UK
UKHW022206230825
462205UK00018B/373